MEMORY SLIPS

a memoir
of music
and healing

SLIPS

Linda Katherine Cutting

HarperPerennial
A Division of HarperCollinsPublishers

Also available on HarperAudio with the author reading and performing music.

A hardcover edition of this book was published in 1997 by HarperCollins Publishers.

HarperCollins books may be purchased for educational, business, or sales promotional use. For information please write: Special Markets Department, HarperCollins Publishers, Inc., 10 East 53rd Street, New York, NY 10022.

First HarperPerennial edition published 1998.

Designed by Laura Lindgren

The Library of Congress has catalogued the hardcover edition as follows:

Cutting, Linda Katherine.
    Memory slips : a memoir of music and healing / Linda Katherine
Cutting — 1st ed.
      p. cm.
   ISBN 0-06-018730-1
    1. Cutting, Linda Katherine. 2. Adult child sexual abuse victims—
United States—Biography.
ML417.C88 A3 1997   97-110403

ISBN 0-06-092879-4 (pbk.)

98 99 00 01 02 ❖/ RRD 10 9 8 7 6 5 4 3 2 1

For my nephew,
Dave

In memory of my brothers,
Paul and David

The strands are all there:
to the memory nothing is ever really lost.

—EUDORA WELTY,
ONE WRITER'S BEGINNINGS

Just as my fingers on these keys
Make music, so the self-same sounds
on my spirit make a music, too.

—WALLACE STEVENS,
"PETER QUINCE AT THE CLAVIER"

ACKNOWLEDGMENTS

Memory Slips passed through so many capable hands on the way to becoming a book. I am more grateful than I can say to those who have helped me on this journey:

My agent, Susan Schulman, who has believed in this book since seeing the first fourteen pages come through her fax machine; my friend Will Ackerman, for sending her those first fourteen pages; my editor, Mitchell Ivers, whose enthusiasm for the writing and careful attention to detail made this book a reality; the Tuesday morning writers' group, which encouraged me through the difficult first drafts of the manuscript—Elizabeth Berg, Sally Brady, Betsy Cox, Alan Emmet, Alex Johnson, Kate Krushwitz, Mary Mitchell, Rick Reynolds, and Donna Stein; the Writers'

Room of Boston for providing a home away from home to write, especially fellow residents Ivan Gold, for helping me believe a book was possible, and Carol Dine, for her crucial edits and encouragement; Steven Ledbetter, for his intelligent editorial advice on writing about music; and Hugh Van Dusen, for his excellent editorial help with the paperback.

Friends and family who read the manuscript and loved and supported me along the way: Eric Brown and Merryl Kaye, Frederick and Mary Ann Brussat, David Allan Cutting, Dr. Margaret Grant, Joanne Cutting-Gray, Shella Harlow, Trix Ingram, Lucia Lin, Keith Lockhart, Maro Lorimer, Sandra Lynn, Judy Nadeau, Daisy Oakley, and Diane Read.

For loving me through all the distractions, and holding my hand to the finish, my husband, Keith William Whited.

CONTENTS

The following names and locales have been changed from their original forms to: Al, Alice, Sherry, Adrienne, Tom, Dr. Thomas, Sarah, Mr. Perch, and Mr. and Mrs. Morgan; Martha's Vineyard, Martha's Vineyard Historical Society, Edgartown Harbor.

PRELUDE

As A CONCERT PIANIST, I've spent years memorizing thousands of pages of music. While the metronome's pendulum swung its beat, the clock's second hand inched away moments. There were moments when music blotted out the rest of my life, but eventually music had to give way to that life, to remembering.

Memory Slips is a memoir of a life lived in music and a life lived between the notes. It includes memories of hundreds of hours of making music. It also includes memories of family violence, incest, and suicide.

The movement from music to writing has been as habitual as daily practicing. While trying to memorize a difficult passage in a Beethoven sonata my mind may suddenly wander to the coffee filters I left off the grocery list, or to the last phone call I had from my sister, or to the long-ago sound of

my brother's trumpet. I have always practiced with a notebook next to the piano, not to remember the music, but to
remember the distractions. I have written daily in these note-
books for more than twenty years. They contain much of the
remembrance of my life.

When I first began writing *Memory Slips* I passed by an
old stone church in Needham, Massachusetts. The sign in
front read, "Memory is where the proof of life is stored." I
looked for the author's name. There was none. Perhaps it was
intended that way, so that those passing by would meditate on
the words alone, understanding that we each author our own
lives.

So much has been done to discredit the memories, and
silence the voices of those who have struggled against great
odds to be heard. Survivors of atrocities, whether they were at
the hands of strangers, trusted clerics, or in the private sanc-
tum of family, do not speak easily of their experiences. They
"long to forget," as Dr. Judith Herman, author of *Trauma and
Recovery,* put it. "But healing requires the reconstruction of
memory; the unspeakable must be spoken and heard."

Survivors don't only forget because of the trauma,
though that in itself would be enough. They forget because
they were told to forget. Whether by threats ("if you tell, I'll
kill you") or by edict ("this did not happen"), reality gets
reshaped.

For me, this reshaping of reality, which began in childhood, continued into adulthood. When I was twenty-seven,

my brother, David, who could no longer fight his own memories of our violent family, shot himself. My parents told the newspapers he'd died in a car accident, and asked me to tell the same story. I refused. I had already lost my oldest brother, Paul, to suicide, and the lie would have made this second grief unbearable. I also promised myself that someday I would write my own story.

In 1992, at a time of deep personal crisis, I met a psychiatrist who had lost most of his family during the Holocaust. He spoke to me of the importance of bearing witness, especially in the face of my brothers' deaths. He then wrote something on a slip of paper, which I have taped above my writing desk: "Stay alive so you can tell." At times, those words have provided the courage to keep on living and writing.

I offer my story in the hope of redemption. That word can mean many things—to recover ownership, to restore honor, to save. I'd like to believe that all of those meanings are at work here—and that as I recover ownership of my own memories, I restore honor to the memory of others who have survived as well as those who haven't.

There were times when the only way for me to stay in life was to cross a river. On the other side there were hands reaching out—friends, teachers, therapists, sisters, other survivors. At times I could have more easily chosen death than attempt that crossing. The courage came in fits and starts—sometimes in a line of music, sometimes in the arms of a loved one, other times in words. When I think of the loneliness of those first steps, a comforting Bible verse I'd memorized as a child returns to me: "When you pass through the waters, I will be with you, and through the rivers, they shall not overwhelm you."

The river is memory. I am standing on the other side. I reach out my hand.

FUGUE

In music, one measure can expand to contain a lifetime. And a lifetime can disappear in just one beat.

The opening eight measures of Beethoven's Sonata in E, opus 109, take about ten seconds to play. Eight seconds if you interpret the "Vivace" to mean very fast. Twelve seconds if you interpret "ma non troppo" as not too fast. The brisk, innocently happy opening gets interrupted in the ninth measure by a menacing diminished seventh chord. By the time you've finished reading this paragraph, the Adagio espressivo should have already begun.

Unless the performer has a memory slip.

In July 1989, on stage, six and a half bars into the opening of the Beethoven, I heard footsteps. Suddenly I was in the wrong key. The footsteps got louder. I tried to go back to the tonic. I couldn't. The footsteps came nearer to the piano. Start again, start the opening, I told myself. I couldn't. Keep your hands on the keys. Impossible. I had to make sure it wasn't him. I stopped, put my hands in my lap, and looked out into the audience.

It was only a latecomer taking his seat. I started again and once I crossed over the diminished seventh chord threshold into the Adagio, I was free. My memory served me through the next seventy minutes of music—the Beethoven, the Bartók Sonata, and Schumann's Fantasy in C. At the end of the Schumann, the audience applauded. I bowed, grateful that the concert was over, unsure if I could ever trust memory again.

There are three kinds of memory slips, I tell my students. One, when memory slips but you find your way back without losing a beat. Two, when you don't find your way back until the downbeat. Three, when you don't find your way back in time and must stop and restart the music.

I don't tell them about a fourth possibility, when one memory slips, another intrudes, and you don't find your way back for a very long time.

It took about seventeen seconds to recover the music I forgot in the Beethoven. It has taken ten years to recover the life I forgot I had lived. The life that began before music or words.

When I sat down at the piano again after almost two years away, the most difficult passages returned—the ones I had spent the most hours practicing: the coda of the second movement of Schumann's Fantasy, with its outward leaps in opposite directions; the fast unison scales at the end of Beethoven's *Emperor* Concerto with the parallel thumb fingering I'd learned to keep the hands exactly together; the end of Bartók's Sonata with the right hand chord clusters bounding back and forth while the left hand marches to a relentless beating drum. Some of the accuracy is lost, and the endurance is not there, but the hours spent choreographing these movements remain in my hands. The muscles retain everything.

My fingertips hold the minutest memories. Practicing on my 1925 Steinway, touching the porous ivory, the memories have stayed in the tips of my fingers—the same way those keys have absorbed moisture. When I bought my 1986 Steinway with its impermeable plastic keys, I missed the way the ivory felt under my fingers. I can still recall the feeling. The only fingertip that doesn't have recall is the one that has lost nerves—fourth finger, left hand. I lost part of that fingertip in August 1987. I'm convinced that some tactile memory was lost with it.

From sleepless nights, I know the muscles remember, too. As a child I spent my nights in vigilance, watching the bedroom door for the crack of light or listening for the sound of footsteps. Though I know in my mind he's not coming into my bedroom tonight, that it's been decades since he last came, my muscles don't know it. Not yet. I am hoping to teach them, the same way I taught them to aim for the faraway note and strike it dead center.

Muscle memory, by itself, is not reliable. The same physical gesture can go more than one way. If you are aroused from sleep by a touch on the shoulder, the muscles may stiffen up in defense. It may take time to understand that a loving gesture in the present is not an assault from the past. By themselves, the muscles can't distinguish. And if the memory of the original gesture has been eclipsed, there is no way to understand the muscles' reactions.

This is certainly true for classical musicians. Classical sonata form demands that the same theme that appears in the opening return at the end of the first movement, but lead to a different key the second time around. A particularly good example of this is Mozart's Piano Concerto no. 23 in A Major, and since it is intended for performance with orchestra, the implications of a memory slip are by definition more harrowing than in performing a solo sonata.

After a long orchestral tutti in the first movement of the Mozart concerto, the piano enters with the bright opening theme. Toward the end of the movement, the identical passage returns and is, note for note, exactly the same until the measure where the left hand plays D-natural instead of D-sharp. All it would take is one missed note—D-sharp instead of D-natural—and the pianist could be playing the beginning of the movement while the orchestra is playing the end.

I performed Mozart's Concerto in A Major in 1983 with the Boston Pops Orchestra, Harry Ellis Dickson conducting. I was well aware of the revered pianists who had performed this piece in Symphony Hall—Alicia de Larrocha, Artur Rubinstein, Rudolf Serkin, to name a few. I was terrified, particularly since the orchestra I was performing with was composed of Boston Symphony members. To add to the tension, I was performing on Alfred Brendel's old Steinway, which Symphony Hall had purchased the year before. Brendel, one of the finest living interpreters of Mozart, had probably played this piece on this very instrument. I didn't want to forget a single note or nuance of my part, and shored up my memory in every possible way—singing and conducting, rehearsing with other pianists playing the orchestra part, even sleeping with the score in case I woke up in a sweat, forgetting some passage.

But it wasn't the piano part that threw me. It was the orchestra. The opening tutti is long, sixty-six measures, but most of my rehearsals had included only the last eight measures before my first entrance. The Boston Pops season is packed—often a different program every night—and rehearsal time is at a premium. I was told that I would probably rehearse with only a string quartet and conductor.

The morning of the performance, however, Harry told me I would get a full orchestra rehearsal, with just enough time to run through a few spots, not the whole concerto. When the orchestra began playing, I was surprised to hear the entire opening tutti unfold. I kept waiting for the music to stop, yet hoped it wouldn't, since I was savoring the sound of that orchestra in that hall as if I were an audience member, not the soloist. When the orchestra played the three quarter notes that end the tutti and signal the beginning of the piano solo, Harry looked at me expectantly. I sat there at Alfred Brendel's Steinway, as if waiting for Brendel himself to start playing. Harry's eyes widened, and I suddenly realized it was I, not Alfred Brendel, who was supposed to come in. I felt the blood rush to my cheeks. Muscle memory would do nothing to help me here. I asked Harry if he could give me the last four bars before my entrance again, and he graciously obliged.

The rest of the rehearsal went without a hitch, but I spent the afternoon with the full score in my lap, studying the opening orchestra tutti, mapping out the entrance of each theme with a letter—A, A1, B, B2, etc., noting whether strings or woodwinds carried the theme, singing and conducting, announcing the key changes out loud. I understand now why so many pianists actually play along in the orchestral sections of Mozart concertos—it's not an egotistical wish to be all things at all times, it's simply a tactile means of helping the memory through the long tuttis. It was too late for me to memorize the orchestra parts at the keyboard. I had to rely on ear and mind to help me remember. I was lucky that night. The orchestra soared. Brendel's piano sang. Memory held.

Muscle memory alone can be as unreliable in life as it is in music. One night my fiancé reached over to touch me, as he often did after I'd fallen asleep. But this time I startled, and all the muscles in my back, neck, and arms tensed as if I were fighting off an attacker. Even fully awake, I couldn't stop shaking, nor could I understand why my body was responding this way. My fiancé was equally bewildered, especially since he'd woken me up in the past and been met with affection.

As misleading as muscle memory can be by itself, I seemed to know in my muscles something I didn't know in my mind—that the night was not for sleeping.

When I was eight, I was a tomboy. I had a brand new baseball bat, a Louisville Slugger, and the bat gave me the power to do more than stand on the sidelines watching my brothers play at Little League games. With a bat, I could join the pick-up games at the field near our house. You could say that I simply loved that bat the way other little girls loved their dolls or stuffed animals. But I slept with that bat. I had a glove, too, and a morning ritual of sinking my nose into the glove's palm to smell the freshly oiled leather. Still, I never slept with my glove. I only slept with my bat. For most of my life I forgot why.

From childhood through adulthood, I needed to sleep with something to protect or comfort me. At twenty, the year after my brother Paul died, I slept with the purple afghan his wife, Sandi, crocheted. At twenty-seven, after my brother David's death, I slept with a T-shirt of his that still smelled like him—sweat mixed with cologne, which he wore in abundance. And at thirty, when my first marriage broke up, I slept with one of my husband's golf clubs, a nine iron. I had no particular affection for the sport. I simply wanted protection. From what or whom, I didn't know.

My muscles were holding their own memories, and I would not sleep through the night for a very long time. Not until I understood what, for so many years, had kept me awake in the dark.

Understanding came with time. After living my life at breakneck speed through my twenties, life slowed down in my thirties, almost coming to a complete stop.

In the first movement of Beethoven's Sonata, op. 109, the opening Vivace is one measure longer than the first Adagio espressivo, yet the Adagio takes about three times as long to play. For the listener, time feels stretched and compressed as the music alternates between these two tempi.

The following narratives, which are ten years apart, mimic the way time is experienced in the first movement of Beethoven's Sonata, op. 109. One narrative spans a year, the other, one month. In the 1982–83 sections, time is moving quickly, even rushing by. In the 1992 sections, time slows down, almost to a standstill.

Time is never strictly chronological in the way it is lived. Musicians know this. Anyone who has ever suffered grief, loss, or a broken heart knows this, too.

I. APRIL–SEPTEMBER 1982/
JULY–AUGUST 1992

AUDITIONS

April *1982.* Schumann Concerto. Orchestra not worth mentioning. What am I doing? This is crazy. On the other hand, what do I have to lose? Where does an unknown pianist in her twenties go after anonymity? Nowhere, which is where I am now. A voice in the distance, my father's—"What are you practicing for? No one will listen to you anyway." John Williams is going to, I say back to the wall. Concertos available: Schumann, Shostakovich's Second, Beethoven's Fifth, MacDowell's Second, and naturally, Gershwin's *Rhapsody in Blue,* the ultimate pops concerto. Available dates: any. Should I admit that? I send a résumé and tape. Express Mail.

July 1992. Suicidal ideation: frequent. Suicide attempts: recent, unsuccessful. Insurance: minimal, friends and family raising the rest. Available dates: any, but sooner would be better than too late. My therapist signs, sends the application. FedEx.

ENGAGEMENTS

May 1982. MAESTRO WILLIAMS WOULD LIKE YOU TO PERFORM SHOSTAKOVICH'S SECOND PIANO CONCERTO WITH THE BOSTON POPS ORCHESTRA JUNE 17. STOP. PLEASE REPLY. STOP.

My mother says my hard work has finally paid off. My father says he's not coming. My mother says she'll come without him.

July 1992. The National Center for the Treatment of Trauma and Dissociation accepts your application. August 2 okay. Dr. Margaret Grant, admitting psychiatrist. Please fax your reply, plus insurance forms.

I haven't spoken to my parents in two years. They send a check anyway. Small, but better than nothing. Friends send the rest.

PRACTICE

June 1982. Third floor, Symphony Hall, piano storage room. Two Steinway nine-foot D's and a Baldwin concert grand. I try the Hamburg Steinway first. The sound is lovely, transparent, mellow, and probably too soft to project over the orchestra. The New York Steinway was Alfred Brendel's, recently purchased by Symphony Hall, completely refurbished. I approach the keyboard a little in awe, find a lovely mellow sound in the middle register, a slightly harsher sound in the upper range. Needs voicing. Repeat not good. Third choice, the Baldwin. It's loud. A bit brassy and bossy sounding. I like that. Gives me a sense of authority I'll need. The repeat is fantastic. But still, it's a Baldwin. I long for the sweet bell-like sound of a Steinway. I try the Hamburg again, then Brendel's old piano, then the Baldwin. Steinway, Steinway, Baldwin, Steinway, Baldwin, Steinway, Baldwin.

My tape recorder is running. I listen back, trying not to let the names of the pianos sway me. Sound, after all, means everything. Still, I want to perform on a Steinway. The Hamburg sounds sweet, way too sweet for this percussive piece, I decide, and too soft. I heard Maurizio Pollini perform the Brahms Second on this piano in the spring. He barely got out over the orchestra. If Pollini couldn't get this piano to project, how could I? No way, Hamburg. Brendel's Steinway is next. It's lovely as long as I'm playing in the middle register, but the lyrical theme of the second movement is all in the upper range. I hear myself miss a few repetitions. Brendel obviously retired this piano with reason. His old Steinway is out. That leaves the Baldwin. The tone is a little too brassy, but bold. I'll have to work for a lyrical legato in the slow movement. The repetition is reliable, rapid as machine gun fire and I know I'll play faster under pressure. I choose the Baldwin, and sit down to run through the whole concerto. There's clapping outside the door. Cleve Morrison, the man who brought me upstairs on the piano elevator, is waiting. He yells "Bravo" then takes me back down.

August 1992. National Center. The cafeteria is empty. The lunch trays have been cleared away. An old upright piano, shrouded in dust, covered with plants, hugs the far wall. Alone, I decide to give it a try. It's been months since I've played. My memory is blank. My fingers are stiff, but they suddenly remember one of Schumann's *Scenes from Childhood* (*Kinderszenen*), "Of Foreign Lands and People." I'm surprised. It's been years since I played that piece. I learned it as a kid. The piano is badly out of tune, not all the keys work, but since I don't remember all the notes anyway, it's fine. It feels good to play. Another one of Schumann's *Scenes from Childhood* returns—"Frightening," and after that, "A Child Falling Asleep." Five bars into the last piece, my memory slips. I can't remember the next chord. Where am I? What age?

Five. I am five and I can't fall asleep. I hear footsteps. Daddy's coming to tuck me in. Please, God, don't let him play those bad games. I am crying. My teeth are chattering. I can't breathe. I'm frozen.

I hear clapping in the distance. The cook comes out of the kitchen. He's walking across the cafeteria toward me. Don't come near me. Don't you dare come near me. Don't touch me. Don't come any closer, I want to scream but can't. He stops. A staff member, Doug, walks through the double doors toward me. Get away, get away, I yell. He squats down beside me. "C'mon," he says, "let's take you back." He extends his hand. I don't take it. He counts slowly from five to one, says we are going back to a safe place. I follow him down the corridors of my mind, then through the locked doors, and back to safety.

REHEARSALS

June 1982. Symphony Hall, second floor. Conductor's green room. Maestro Williams greets me warmly, suggests I call him John. He is more gracious than I could have imagined and this puts me at ease. I sit down at the Baldwin and open my score. He opens his. We talk about tempo, then start the first movement. He sings the orchestra tuttis; I play my solos. In the second movement, he asks me how long I want to trill. A French horn accompanies me there, sustaining a long G. I play the trill. The second and fourth fingers of my right hand buzz like a hummingbird's wings, then gradually slow down and continue the line. I'm amazed that I can go on this way— maybe it's nerves that make me trill longer and faster than usual, maybe it's my chance to show off, or maybe it's what I want for the music. I'm not sure. But John smiles at me and says, "I'll get the horn player to take a breath just before the trill so he can stay with you." I'm grateful and just hope I can pull it off on stage, under pressure.

August 1992. National Center. Cafeteria. I must be accompanied at all times now. My friend Sherry, and Nancy, a staff member, stay with me. The lunch trays have been cleared. I ask if they mind if I play—just a few minutes before our next group, called "Breaking Silence." They both nod as if they've been waiting for this, and I tell them I'm rusty and please don't expect much. My fingers find "Of Foreign Lands and People" again, "Catch Me," then "Frightening," and finally "A Child Falling Asleep." I get to the end this time without flashbacks—all the way to an unresolved minor chord which I hold until the sound is finally gone. I'm amazed that I can go on this way, as if my fingers remember what my mind has shut off. More scenes from my own childhood return, but I remember them this time without going back so far that I can't return on my own. Now I am six. Daddy buys me a piano and we strike our first deal—if I keep quiet, he'll let me have lessons, as long as I'm practicing, he'll leave me alone. I hug the piano, sing "Ollie, ollie in free, no one can get me."

Now I am sixteen. I'm playing loud and fast. Bartók's *Allegro Barbaro* becomes Emerson, Lake, and Palmer's *The Barbarian* and I have something to play that my friends can relate to. My father is shouting. I play louder and faster. He's shouting at my brother, Paul, and hits him. I play still louder, still faster. I am the barbarian. No, he is the barbarian. I slam the chords into the keys and hope my brother hits him back. My biology book is open next to the music. I'm studying for a biology test, trying to memorize the structure of the DNA molecule and *Allegro Barbaro* at the same time. As long as the music doesn't stop, I can concentrate on both, and block out the yelling.

Another *Scene from Childhood* returns, "The Knight of the Hobby Horse." I play it fast and furious for Sherry, who claps and says go on, go on, but Nancy lets us know it's time for group.

Breaking Silence is not so hard today. Sherry and I both keep down lunch.

CONCERTS

June 1982. Symphony Hall, first floor. There's a knock on the door of my dressing room. "Five minutes," Cleve, the stage manager, calls. I race out into the hallway backstage and warm up for a last few minutes on the Baldwin, then watch as it is rolled out onto the stage. John comes down the steps from his dressing room, takes both my hands in his, and asks, "Are you ready?" I nod, hoping I look more ready than I feel, and he sends me out on stage in front of him. I hear the sound of my feet on the wooden floor as I walk the narrow passage through the orchestra, then the reassuring stomps of the musician's feet, and finally the deafening thunder of nearly three thousand pairs of hands. I look out in the audience, knowing my mother and even my father are there, but unable to see them with the stage lights blinding me. I sit down on the bench, grasp the round knobs on either side and pretend to adjust them. I'm buying time for my heart to stop racing. John looks my way and waits for my cue. I nod and the orchestra begins.

There's more noise in the audience than I'd counted on,

and some woman in the first row of tables is pouring a drink from a pitcher. I try to block this out, but she's still pouring and my entrance is coming in three more bars. Oh God, don't let my memory slip, I pray. I begin to play. I'm eighteen bars in, and the sweat is already beading up on my forehead. That woman is still pouring water. My God, is she going to fill glasses for the entire audience? I want to kick her, she's almost close enough, but my foot is glued to the pedal. In the fifty-third bar my memory slips—F becomes A—and I improvise. One measure is a thousand years until memory returns.

Now there is only the music—my own, and the orchestra's. There's nothing like this—when only the music exists, propelling forward into time, yet timeless, stretching the present into eternity. Everything else fades into the background leaving the feeling of dancing on the keys, the sound of an orchestra that's like no other orchestra in the world, surrounding and coloring every note, arriving in the hot center of the beat at exactly the same moment the hammer strikes the strings. There's John at the helm, steady and sure of himself, making me feel that I can do anything and he will see to it that the orchestra is with me.

I feel a surge of strength in my arms, and the athlete's thrill of my body reaching its peak, its stride. I don't want this to end—I'm balancing at the tip of this peak it's taken years to ascend—but soon my hands are leaping over each other in a cascade of descending arpeggios. The full orchestra has the theme now, and we're traveling fast toward the cadenza.

I don't remember what happens after that, except John Williams takes me by the hand and leads me on and off stage for curtain calls. There are four, and a standing ovation. My husband, Dan, hands me a dozen white roses.

Still, in the middle of the night, I wake up crying over a memory slip.

August 1992. National Center. Cafeteria. The old upright piano is waiting. I've promised the whole trauma unit a concert tonight, to break up the long, dull weekend. Big Al, from the weekend nursing pool, says it's time to leave. I guess no concert after all. Like obedient dogs, we all stand up, except Sherry, who sits at the table and crosses her toothpick arms across her chest.

"I'm not leaving until after the concert," she says.

Big Al's eyes widen. Unrehearsed, but right on cue, we all sit.

"I'm sorry, but I have to take you back to the unit," Al says. He is sweating. We like that in a staff member.

"Fine," says Sherry, who walks over to the piano and, with a sudden power surge, lifts a five-foot hibiscus off the top. "But the piano goes with us."

In a heartbeat we're up, clearing off ropy philodendrons.

"Now wait just a minute," Big Al protests.

"Don't pee your pants about it," says Sherry, who is already leaning into the piano with every bit of her eighty-eight pounds and pushing. "We've got a requisition."

Sherry's powers of improvisation amaze me.

"You do?" Al scratches his bald spot. Sherry has lost twenty pounds in three weeks, but still has dazzling red hair and green eyes to die for. He looks at her and we watch his resolve begin to melt.

"Of course," Adrienne adds. "We voted at the community meeting this morning and the big chief gave her okay."

We all laugh, except Al.

"C'mon, Al, this thing is heavy," says Sherry. "Give us a hand."

Big Al comes around and takes Sherry's place behind the piano. "Okay, but it goes right back to the cafeteria tonight," Al says, and gives the piano a shove.

Soon we're outside the cafeteria, rolling the piano down the long corridor. Big Al unlocks the first, the second, then the third set of locked double doors. The piano glides through.

I'm feeling an odd sensation of pressure. What if we get this piano all the way there, and I can't remember a note of what I'm supposed to play? I used to dream about forgetting the music, standing up and doing a comedy routine instead. I was voted "best sense of humor" in high school. But I don't feel funny tonight.

"How do we get this past the nurses' station?" Adrienne whispers.

"Leave it to me," Sherry whispers back, then races ahead to the nurses' station and steps onto the scale. The med nurse who mans the station is on her like a vulture, trying to pull her off. Sherry is grasping the post with one hand, trying to move the sliding weight with the other.

"Sherry, if you don't get off that scale, we're going to drop your privs. You're breaking your contract."

"I don't care," she yells, and we roll the piano past the nurses' station and through the door into the smoking lounge.

Now I'm sitting at the piano, smoke billowing like clouds around me. The whole room is quiet and I know I need to remember Schumann's *Scenes from Childhood*—not just for myself, but for every woman here who has lost hers.

"Of Foreign Lands and People" comes back, then "Pleading Child," followed by "Perfect Happiness," "Frightening," then "Dreaming." I've left out a few, but I hold the unresolved minor chord of "A Child Falling Asleep" until it disappears.

JUNE 1982, BOSTON

Monday morning after the Boston Pops concert, a colleague of mine from Northeastern University calls. Apparently, John Williams was just awarded an honorary doctorate at New England Conservatory. Robin was his personal chauffeur.

"We talked about recent soloists," she says, taking a long drag from her cigarette.

I wait for her to exhale, pressing the phone hard against my ear.

" 'Finest young talent I've heard this year,' " Williams said.

"Who?" I ask, trying to breathe in unison with her, unable to exhale. I wonder if it's the incredible Russian pianist who played Rachmaninoff's Second with the Pops a few weeks ago.

"You."

"What?" All the air I've been sucking in comes out at once. I was waiting for her to tell me he'd said something about the memory slip.

"You just don't know how good you are."

"Robin, I screwed up just fifty measures into the performance—I was lucky to get through it."

"Maybe, but if you work hard and keep family crises out of your life, you may have a career."

The next day, my father and I are driving my husband Dan's mother and grandmother to the airport. Gram, who's eighty years old, flew all the way from Spokane, Washington, to hear me perform. Also to inspect the century-old Victorian house we bought in Newton with the help of Dan's father.

"It's not as bad as I thought it would be," she says as we pull out of the driveway. I don't ask what she'd imagined it would look like. I'm just happy she came. She is the only grandmother I have right now. My grandmother on my father's side died when I was thirteen. My grandmother on my mother's side died a few weeks ago. I had to choose between attending the funeral and playing this concert.

Dan's mother came, too. If I hadn't married her son, I

would have had to find some other way to keep her in my life. I am closer to Mil (short for mother-in-law) than I am to my own mother, and it makes me feel a little guilty. Before she was my mother-in-law, Margaret Ott was my piano teacher in college. She has a knack for pushing her students way beyond where they think they can go. She was the one who suggested I audition for John Williams.

"What do you have to lose?" she'd said. I couldn't think of anything at the time, so I sent the tape.

At the airport, I hug Mil and Gram good-bye, then watch as the two of them disappear down the walkway, leaving me alone with my father.

On the way back from the airport my father clears his throat, adjusts his glasses.

"This concert was one of the most thrilling events in my life."

I can't believe it. He almost didn't come. Yet even after a standing ovation from nearly three thousand people in Symphony Hall, it's still my father I want to impress.

"Really?"

"Of course, you could have performed that concerto when you were fifteen."

I swerve right, almost miss my exit, and downshift hard into third gear.

"What do you mean?"

"Your driving could stand a little improvement—"

"I mean about the Shostakovich—"

"You could have played it with the Cheyenne Symphony—"

"I did play with the Cheyenne Symphony. It was MacDowell, not Shostakovich, and I was seventeen, not fifteen."

My father looks at himself in the mirror and smooths his hair back, what's left of it.

"If you hadn't been on drugs, you could have won the Cheyenne Symphony Young Artists Competition two years earlier."

I clutch the steering wheel remembering how one of my father's parishioners who was fixing my VW Beetle found Zigzag rolling papers in the back seat. They weren't even mine. Still, I must have smoked dope six or seven times, and I was sixteen, not fifteen. Not long afterward, during one of his sermons, my father had confessed to the whole congregation that his daughter was doing drugs. I remember slinking down as low as I could into my pew, the object of God's and my father's wrath.

"Our church choir director said you were the clear winner. And he ought to have known—he was the symphony conductor."

The heat in the car is unbearable. I roll down my window and step on the gas. The rest of the way home we are silent.

When we pull into the driveway, my mother walks out to the car waving a piece of paper and hands it to me. There's a number scrawled across it.

"John Williams's secretary, Nancy, called," Mom says between breaths. She has trouble breathing when she gets excited. I must get that from her.

My mother is beaming, until she looks at my father.

"What's wrong, Harvey? Are you two at it again?"

I jump out of the car, take the phone number, and call.

It turns out John Williams wants me to come back and perform the Shostakovich in the last two Symphony Hall concerts. I'm ecstatic, and terrified. I tell Nancy I've scheduled a trip, that I'll have to think about it.

But really, I am stalling the way I do on stage just before the performance begins, when I pretend to adjust the knobs on the bench while waiting for my heart's wild beat to slow down.

That night, after Dan comes home from work, I tell him the news. He is not happy.

"What about our vacation?" he says. "We're scheduled to fly to Spokane for ten days. We've been looking forward to this."

"I haven't said yes."

I spend the night staring into Dan's back. Please talk to me, hold me, something. If I say yes will I lose you? If I say no will I lose the chance to perform with the Pops again?

The next morning John Williams's office calls. They offer to fly me back from Spokane for the concerts.

A compromise. No rehearsal, but I can have part of my vacation and still do the concerts.

Two weeks later, on the flight from Spokane to Boston, I think about the question Dan's mother asked me, "What do you have to lose?" I have a sinking feeling I might know the answer.

The vacation was tense. The last few days, Dan was a stone wall. He's angry that I'm doing these performances, that I'm leaving early. Until now, he's been my main support. I feel like I'm losing my best friend.

It's strange to walk off a plane in Boston knowing my husband won't be there at the gate. Peppino, the Boston Symphony's chauffeur, with his raven black hair, dancing brown eyes, and a smile that wins over the most jet-lagged guest conductors and soloists, is waiting instead.

"Greetings, Signora," he says, leading me by the elbow into his gray-black limo. I feel a little less lonely. We head straight to Symphony Hall.

Since there's not going to be a rehearsal, I hope the orchestra remembers the tempo changes and cues. I hope I remember the music. I'm carrying the pale pink silk gown Dan's mother and grandmother bought me. It's straight and simple with a tiny slit up the front so I can pedal. It's soft, so it won't make noise during the *pianissimos* like the red taffeta I wore for the first concert. This dress makes me feel like part of Dan's family is with me, even if he isn't. If I were a man, I'd just wear the same tux night after night. Everything would be simpler.

Backstage, my heart is pounding. John Williams welcomes me, takes both my hands in his. He's wearing a different jacket. Maroon brocade. It's a good thing I'm not wearing red.

"I'm so glad you're here," he says. His smile is like oxygen. I start to breathe easier. The door opens. We walk out on stage.

I adjust the bench, nod to John, and wait for the downbeat. I look out under the raised piano lid at the viola section. The jackets are a different color, white instead of gray. There are no familiar faces. Four bars before my entrance, I realize this is not the same orchestra I performed with two weeks ago.

I look down at the keyboard. This, at least, is familiar. Before my first performance with the Pops, I'd had a lesson with Leonard Shure. I remember asking him how he dealt with the anxiety of performing in Symphony Hall the first time. He'd performed the Brahms D Minor with Koussevitsky. He must have been about my age.

"All those statues peering down at you from above, and all those faces staring up at you from the audience—"

Leonard lit a cigarette, took a couple of drags.

"My dear," he said in his most exasperated tone, "what do you think you'll be looking at when you play? Statues? Maybe you look at those when you are sitting in the audience. On stage you'll be looking at this—" he pointed to the keyboard. "Eighty-eight keys, black and white. It will look just the same as it looks now. Remember that."

I remember it now, and once I am playing, I forget the jackets, I forget the faces. The French horn waits for me at the end of my trill in the slow movement. In the third movement sections that sound like Hanon finger exercises, the timpani is steady as a heartbeat.

Backstage, in my dressing room, I check the program. Right away I recognize the names of some of Boston's best freelancers. This is the Boston Pops Esplanade Orchestra, the backup band for the Boston Symphony players who are starting their summer season at Tanglewood. There's a note under the door. I open it.

"Bravo—you've come a long way since Harvest. Love, Dave."

Dave Brown. My first major crush in college. I can't believe he's here. We played in a rock group called Harvest. Dave played lead guitar, sang, and wrote the few original songs we performed. He's the only guy besides my brother, Paul, who could get me to sing and play the piano at the same time. I refold the note, run a brush through my hair, and wait for the knock that I hope will be his.

For the final concert I wear the red taffeta. Feeling less afraid poses a new problem—how to keep my concentration when I'm not driven by fear. My whole life I've been driven by fear. Playing the piano has been one way of dealing with it. I'm not sure what I'll do when the fear is gone. There's no time to think about it now. We are ending the slow movement. In a few minutes this will all be over.

The twelve repeated unison Cs that begin the third movement are slower than usual, and I'm distracted, thinking about Dan. Can I admit I've enjoyed doing these concerts without him? Can you love your work this much and still have the other kind of love? What if your work is your first love?

My fingers seem to be traveling without me tonight. I'm not fully present. I want to go home, but I'm not sure where home is—here, with the music, or with Dan.

We're approaching the first 7/8 passage and I want the orchestra to crescendo with me, but this morning I saw the orchestra parts. They were marked "sordino" and "*pianissimo*" throughout the strings. Why didn't I say something? Now it's too late. No matter how much I crescendo here, I do it alone.

There's a burst of applause at the end, but I hear it from a distance, the way you hear the cheers at a football stadium while driving by.

Backstage, I receive bravos, hugs, and slaps on the back. I force out a smile and nod thank you to the musicians walking by, but I just want to disappear. Harry Ellis Dickson, the associate conductor, asks me to send him a repertoire list for next year.

"I'd be honored," I say.

I walk up the steps to my dressing room, close the door, kick off my shoes, and curl up into a ball on the couch. A red taffeta ball.

There's a knock on the door. I sweep my hands through my hair, wipe the mascara rings from under my eyes, and open the door. Cleve, the stage manager, greets me with a tray—two Heinekens and two roast beef sandwiches. He looks around the room, which is empty, except for my rumpled street clothes and the concerto score, and sets the tray down on my dressing table. I thank him, but don't have the heart to tell him I'm not hungry, that there's no one joining me.

I look at the clock on the wall. I'm late. Dan's plane is landing. I peel off my gown, throw on some shorts, turn off the lights in my dressing room, slide my name card out of the bracket on the door, grab my flowers, and run down the stairs to the stage door. I feel like Cinderella at midnight, except I'm wearing Nikes instead of slippers.

"Goodnight, Signora," Peppino says.

He won't be driving me in the limo tonight. I'm tempted to leave one shoe behind, just for him.

I throw all my stuff into the back seat of the Volvo. Pulling out of the soloist's spot in front of the stage door, I squeal my tires, leave some rubber.

On the way to the airport, I think about getting pregnant.

AUGUST 1992, DENVER

"The piano must go back," we are told the morning after my concert in the smoking lounge. Everyone moans. Sherry, naturally, is the first to speak up.

"We need the piano. We need live music. We go to therapy, we go to groups. It gets boring around here."

"Yeah," says Adrienne. "Music therapy."

Everyone laughs, except me. I wrote a paper in college on music therapy. It's been proven effective with autistic children. Why not here?

"The piano goes back," Marion says in that I'm-not-tak-ing-any-more-shit tone of voice.

"Give us one more day." Leave it to Sherry to push past Marion's limits.

"Fine. Today. But it goes back tonight."

I sneak out of the meeting and into the smoking lounge. I want to be with the piano alone before it goes back and remem-ber my other life. My life in music has all but disappeared.

I've spent so much time in the way back—in the life that was mine before I learned to play the piano—that I've lost hold of the life I've had since. I need both to be whole.

I stroke the keys without making a sound. They are plas-tic, chipped here and there. A few cigarette burns mar middle C. I place my index finger on middle C and strike it lightly, then again, then a third time, a fourth, and a fifth. When I am up to seven, I stop, then play seven more. I know I am playing the piece my first piano teacher assigned me, the one I prac-ticed with my mother sitting beside me on the bench. It is the old Sunday school piano in the Baltimore church where my father was minister.

"I-am-mis-ter-mid-dle-C, take-a-good-long-look-at-me."

Even at the age of six I thought it was a stupid song. I could already play many more notes, but I was learning to read music in that silly way they used to teach kids—when the world revolved around middle C. Middle C looked like Saturn on the page—a circle with a line through it. I knew even then that the world didn't revolve around Saturn. It revolved around my mother and trying to please her, doing anything I could that would keep her near me.

I remember repeating middle C again and again, asking my mother if it sounded all right, not wanting her to move an inch from my side. I didn't want to practice in the church without her. But too quickly I got better at the piano than she, and was left to practice at the church without her.

I begged for a piano so I could practice at home. If I could practice at home I'd be safe. I could call out to my mother and she would hear me. In the church, she couldn't hear me. My father could.

I didn't realize the power of the repeated C until years later when I began learning Beethoven's *Waldstein* Sonata. There are sixteen repeated Cs in the opening two measures. They gather tremendous tension before moving to B, then the B gathers tension before moving to B-flat, then A, then A-flat, and finally to the dominant, G. I begin playing the opening now, C major beating like an infant heart, *pianissimo*, until eleven measures later it explodes into *forte*.

I hear the door swish open. It's Deb, my favorite nurse. She smiles at me, says it's beautiful, but could I please keep it down. I need this time alone, and she understands.

I go back to middle C, repeat it fourteen more times, whispering "I am mister middle C, take a good long look at me."

If only my mother could see me now.

AUGUST 1982, ASPEN

I'm practicing in the big wooden rehearsal building on the pond. The glass sliding doors open to a deck overlooking the water, the wooden doors to the mountainside. You can hear the birds chirping their morning song, and feel the cool alpine breeze on your face. It's almost like practicing outside, something string and wind players do all the time. I've gone for runs on the path behind the practice cabins and on the way up the mountain I've bumped into flutists, violinists, and clarinetists, their music stands set up in patches of mountain heather or Indian paintbrush. Practicing the piano can be so confining, especially on a beautiful, sunny day, which, in Aspen, is almost every day. I've always been jealous of musicians who can take their instruments outside.

I'm working on Schumann's *Fantasy Pieces*, *op.12* (*Fantasiestücke*) to perform for Claude Frank's master class. I've idolized Claude Frank and his wife, Lilian Kallir, since my early days as a student here. They are two of the kindest musicians I know, both outstanding pianists in their own right, and on top of it all, they are raising a musically well-adjusted daughter, a young violinist named Pamela. I dream they are my parents.

But since they are not, and since I'm playing for Claude Frank tomorrow, I need to work on the music. The first piece, "Evening", is in 3/8 but the sixteenths divide rather neatly into duplets in the left hand. How do I capture the rhythmic tension of three against two without interrupting the delicate right-hand melody? It's a problem. Getting a legato line in the right hand is already a problem.

The skips are so large between the melody, which is mostly in the fourth and fifth fingers, and the accompanying notes, which are all in the thumb. That demon thumb.

There is such utter calm in this piece, despite the tension. How did Schumann get that? Maybe he wrote it in early evening, while watching the sunset. Surely his piano was near a window. All pianos should be, no matter what technicians say about outer walls. If I find a practice room here where the piano is not near the natural light source, I ignore the Do Not Move sign and roll it over to the window.

I learned this irreverence in college. The whole piano department was working on Beethoven's *Emperor* Concerto for a competition. We were all sick of the hours we had to spend practicing inside while the English majors read outside under trees. One sunny afternoon, we rolled an upright out the double doors of the music building and into the parking lot. We took turns playing excerpts from every piece of music we'd ever memorized. Colette, a mere freshman, outlasted us all. She'd grown up with seven siblings and two pianos. Simultaneous practicing was the norm. She'd had to practice with a rarefied focus, like looking down the barrel of a shotgun, and the pieces she'd memorized as a kid just never left her. Margaret Ott, our piano teacher, and the only faculty member whose approval mattered, flashed us a smile on the way out to her car. But a music theory professor followed

right on her heels and demanded we stop. Colette kept playing, drowning out the professor's voice with the demonic
Scarbo by Ravel.

The musician's need to get outdoors is probably the reason there are so many music festivals set in the most beautiful
parts of the world. The Aspen Music Festival is no exception.
You have to head up the mountain past wildflower meadows
and the Prince of Peace chapel to get to the main campus, and
the Roaring Fork River runs right behind the practice cabins.
No mistake in that. You have to arrive early to get one of
those. But no matter where I am, or what music I'm practicing, I stop to watch the sun go down. All the mountain tops
are bathed in a pale pink glow.

There are so many distractions here, the good kind, but
now I have rolled the piano right next to the open wooden
doors, so I'm almost outside. Back to the Schumann. The hardest of the eight *Fantasy Pieces* is no. 5, "In the Night." By the
third measure the right hand begins its tormenting theme in
three while the left hand continues in four. The three against
four is not especially difficult—it flies swiftly by. Too swiftly at
times, and that is the problem. When I am really playing this
figure well, so the tension is strong until the downbeat, and the
eighth rest feels like a gasp for air, I feel a terror inside that
makes me want to push even faster. It's a tribute to Schumann's
genius as a composer that in the stroke of seven eighth notes
followed by an eighth rest he can strike terror into your heart.
But the terror makes me want to play faster.

It reminds me of Schumann's Sonata in G Minor, which I performed in a master class in Aspen years ago. I was studying with Aube Tzerko then, who had been a student of the brilliant but demanding pianist and pedagogue, Artur Schnabel. (Leonard Shure and Claude Frank had also studied with Schnabel, whose reputation for his sadistic treatment of students was almost as well-known as his brilliant interpretations of Beethoven sonatas.) I was playing the last movement, which is marked "presto" (very fast), then "prestissimo" (faster still), then finally, "*Immer schneller und schneller*" (always faster and faster). I remember playing at what I thought was my top speed, while Tzerko yelled "faster, faster," like a horse trainer with a whip. I kept playing faster, then faster still, all the while wondering if I could stay on the horse. When I finished, Tzerko nodded his head and said, "Well, apparently not all the good pianists are from New York." After the master class I went back to my practice cabin and cried my eyes out, not knowing why.

I've always loved speed. Fast motorcycles, fast cars, a steep hill on my skis or my bike. But I've always known there was terror behind it. In ninth grade I ran the 440-yard dash in a smooth 56.4, setting the unofficial Wyoming state record. Wyoming is a state with more cows than people, so it wasn't such a big deal. But I remember feeling like a fraud, because I ran that race out of sheer terror. A ninth-grade girl from the other junior high in Cheyenne was running the race. The last time I'd seen her was from the opposite side of the volleyball net for a tournament. I'd blocked five out of seven of her spikes and our team won. I was tall for my age, five foot eight inches, but she towered over me at six foot two. At the start of the race, our cleats in the start blocks, our butts in the air, she whispered to me "If I catch you I'm gonna beat the ever-living shit out of you." The gun went off and I ran faster than I'd ever run in my life, or would ever run again. I quit track after that meet.

So my problem with "In the Night" is this: How do I create the terror in this piece without scaring myself into a too-fast tempo? Three pages from the end, Schumann writes "*nach und nach immer schneller*" (little by little always faster), and if I am already playing at my top speed, I'm in trouble. How do I let this figure run wild, yet control it enough to hang on, then play even faster toward the end?

Schumann must have had night terrors. I know I do. They run in my family. My brother David has been calling me long-distance in the middle of the night. He figures it's two hours earlier where I am, so if he calls me at two A.M. Florida time, it's midnight in Colorado. He works at a nuclear power plant that's under construction, and now he's working the graveyard shift six days a week. Something's really wrong. He doesn't say that, but I can tell by his voice.

In July he wrote me a letter congratulating me on my concerts with the Boston Pops. He said he showed the program to everyone at work and did a lot of bragging about his sister. He went on to write, "Your musical prowess is only exceeded by your brother's good looks!" So typical of my brother David, who spent more time in the bathroom combing his hair than my mother, my sister, and myself combined. But his latest letter worries me. There are no jokes, and he writes down his telephone number in case I don't have it in Aspen, asks me to call. He knows I am working hard on my music, he says, but "don't burn yourself out."

He is the one burning out. I can tell by the way he writes about his job. He's supposed to be doing safety checks on this nuclear power plant, but his employer has a deadline to meet, so he's under pressure to keep quiet about what he sees. But it's his safety I'm worried about. I don't know how he's going to make it through the nights.

I wonder how Schumann did. Maybe that's when he wrote most of his music. When he jumped off the bridge into the Rhine River, was that late at night?

I call my parents to say I am worried about David. He sounds depressed. "You're making mountains out of molehills," my mother says. "David just hasn't adjusted to the graveyard shift yet."

"You're still not over Paul's death," my father says. "That's what's wrong."

"Maybe you're right," I say, and hang up the phone, not reassured. I think about Paul, about how he would love this place. He loved the mountains. Taught me to ski, both downhill and cross-country. "You have to fall a lot, Lindi," he'd say. "It means you're learning." At sixteen I stopped believing him.

We were skiing Steamboat Springs on a black diamond slope called Concentration. A huge rock jutted out near the end of the run. Paul took that jump every time, sucking the tails of his skis up to his back, sailing into the air like a wingless bird, then disappearing into a cloud of white. He missed the landing every time. He wasn't learning.

I wish Paul could visit me here. We could climb the Maroon Bells together. We climbed our first fourteener (fourteen thousand foot peak) when I was ten, David was twelve, and Paul was fourteen. Horn Peak in the Sangre de Cristo Mountains. I'll never forget that first ascent—the thrill of making it above treeline, the endless jagged rocks to the top, the panoramic view four states wide, then the long slide down the glacier.

Instead of Paul, his widow, Sandi, is coming to visit me in Aspen. Her new husband, Tom, is coming with her. She's six months pregnant. We're going to take the Aspen Highlands lift to the top and walk down. I hope she'll be okay with that baby inside her. She's due in November.

In December, it will be seven years since Sandi found Paul hanging from a beam in the garage behind their house.

My parents are right. I'm still not over it.

Tonight I can't sleep. I'd blame it on anxiety about the master class, but I haven't slept well since I got here. I'd blame it on the high altitude, but I've spent too many years of my life living above six thousand feet. I've never slept well. My mother says I'm a night owl. She can't bring herself to call me an insomniac. My father and my brother David are insomniacs. My brother Paul had trouble sleeping, too, until he decided to sleep forever.

The thing is, I hate to waste time. If I could practice I wouldn't mind not sleeping, but there are no buses up to the school this late, and I'm too tired to ride my bike up the hill. The worst thing is lying in bed staring at the ceiling. That's when I'm loneliest. That's when my mind goes blank. I could call Dan, but it's two hours later in Boston. I try to imagine him lying in our bed, sleeping soundly, but my mind is already blank. Home has disappeared again. It happens every time I go away. My therapist says I have problems with object constancy. The only constant in my life is the piano and if I can't get to one I panic. She suggested I take some photographs with me on this trip to help me remember home. I forgot to bring them.

I try to remember home, what it feels like, but I can't. I take out my notebook and draw my house. I draw flower boxes in all the windows and surrounding the deck. If I hadn't come to Aspen, I would have planted flowers. Why didn't I stay home? I was ambivalent about coming to Aspen, but the dean at Northeastern had written me a travel grant. I felt obligated.

I draw my house the way it looks now, stripped of its old front porch, then I draw a new front porch, and the clapboard siding we're hoping to restore some day. I draw the yard, the shrubs that line the deck, the two rhododendron bushes that flank the front entrance, and the tall scotch pine that protects the house from too much sun.

It doesn't help. I can draw the details, but I can't remember living there. It's not real. It's just pencil lines on a page. I'm having trouble breathing. Can't seem to get enough air. Why do I feel so detached from everyone and everything I love?

My parents sent me a letter today. They're thinking of moving again. This will be their fifth move in eight years. I don't even want to write back. Every time they move something awful happens. The year they moved from Cheyenne, Wyoming, to Dallas, Texas, Paul hanged himself. The year they moved from Dallas to Milton, Connecticut, my mother was so depressed she'd just stare off into the empty spaces of their new house, unable to move a muscle. When my parents moved from Connecticut to Green Bay, Wisconsin, my therapist moved, my brother David and his wife and kid moved, my best friend from grad school moved, and Dan and I moved. I started unraveling. It was just too many losses on top of the still massive grief about my brother Paul's suicide.

My breathing is getting more shallow. I can't get enough air. It's two A.M. I decide to wake Dan. I dial the number and listen for the ring. Please answer, please. Finally, a half-awake hello.

"What's going on?"

"I forgot to bring the pictures."

"What time is it?"

"Late—could you walk around the house and make some familiar sounds?"

I hear him sigh loudly into the phone and throw off the sheet. That helps a little. I can almost see the bed.

"What do you want to hear?"

"How about the squeaky kitchen drawer?"

He puts down the phone and picks up the one in the kitchen. I hear the drawer squeak, and it starts to appear in my mind, like a Polaroid photo developing.

"That helps." Dan opens the refrigerator door. I'm starting to see more of the kitchen. I hear the light click on inside the refrigerator, and I imagine Dan's face illuminated. He turns on the faucet. I start to see his hand, then his arm.

"That's good. Keep going—"

He slams a few cupboards. I hear the toaster oven bell ring, a chair skidding across the floor. I have the whole kitchen now, and most of Dan.

"Could you pick up the phone in the living room?"

I hear the receiver hit the kitchen counter top, then footsteps. I hear Dan pick up the other phone, the one near the piano.

"Okay."

"Could you just play a few notes?"

I hear middle G twice, then E, then A, then G again. It sounds like one of the Bartók pieces for children, *Serenade*. I've lived with my husband for six years, and only now realize what a beautiful sound he gets from the piano. Maybe it sounds beautiful because it's my piano, or maybe I'm remembering what it's like to be home.

I'm starting to feel sleepy, and Dan is beginning to sound like he's ski instructing, which is what he did in Vail for two years before we moved to Boston.

"You have to feel that outside edge—" it means he's falling asleep on the phone.

I wake up to a string quartet rehearsal next door. Sounds like Beethoven, one of the *Razumovsky* quartets. I must have slept through the night without hanging up. The receiver is dangling from its cord beside the bed. A small but expensive connection if Dan forgot to hang up, too.

Another dream about a dark-haired man. I think he was a boyfriend of my best friend in college. We were part of a hospital experiment where they randomly selected people to have sex with each other, to measure the responses of sexual experience without emotional responsibility. But since the man whose name they drew was my best friend's boyfriend, I couldn't do it without feeling emotionally responsible. I suppose I must have been attracted to this guy at some point, because even though my friend married someone else, I feel guilty about this dream.

The master class goes well, or so I'm told. The Arab woman who runs the music store says Claude Frank stopped by after class and told her what a pleasure it was to work with someone so musical who had really thought out every detail of the Schumann. I thank her for telling me, but I don't remember any details of what I just did. I feel like my hands played without me again. But maybe the practice is paying off.

If I can't stay conscious during the performance, I can at least consciously work out the details in practice. They seem to stick while I'm playing. But if you can't remember what you just did and someone tells you it went well, you feel like a fake. Still, the music doesn't lie. You have to play the notes and you can't fake the feeling. I'm glad I remembered the music. I just can't remember how the performance went.

Nothing sticks inside me, not my house, my husband, performing, nothing. I'm twenty-seven. I ought to feel like I exist in the world. I only exist in the music. When I stop playing, everything vanishes.

Home is disappearing again. Sandi is coming to visit tomorrow. Maybe that will help. And I still have a lesson with Kallir at the end of the week. I have to start practicing for that.

I'm working on Beethoven's *Waldstein* Sonata. There is such utter joy in the third movement, I'm not sure I can touch it. After the relentless intensity of the first movement and the dark, foreboding harmonies of the second, there's this impossible clearing to C major. It's like a clear blue sky after storm clouds have parted. Beethoven did the same thing in the *Pastoral* Symphony, even indicated it in the last movement with words—"thankful feelings after the storm" or something like that. But I think he does it better in the last movement of this sonata. The question is, can I do it? Such unearned joy, and I don't think it will feel any more earned after hours and weeks of practice. It is simply a gift.

Another problem—how to get my clunky hands to play this ethereal theme without any bumps or accents? The opening theme is long—thirty-two bars. The pedal will help. Beethoven marked a sustained pedal through ten measures. Impossible to bring off on the modern piano. Maybe only possible on Beethoven's Broadwood piano with its threadlike strings. Still, the composer marked it. I know what Shure would say if I asked him—"Do you think you know better than Beethoven how to pedal this passage?" I don't, but I'm uncomfortable holding down the pedal through all those harmonic changes, overtones ringing from all the open strings, vibrating like hundreds of church bells.

I could cheat a little, take a few half pedals, let the dampers slip way down, hover just above the vibrating strings, almost touching, but not quite touching.

I wonder what Kallir does. I'm sure she'll tell me at my lesson, but I'm at a stage in my career when I ought to know what I'm doing before I get someone else's opinion.

Kallir is the first woman I've studied with who has a major performing career. In fact, that's mostly what she does. She teaches very little. I'm lucky to be one of the few students she takes. I've studied with two incredibly competent, inspiring women—Patricia Zander at the New England Conservatory, and before that, in college, with Margaret Ott, who is now my mother-in-law. Why is it so crucial for me to study with a woman who is an established performing artist? I need permission to do this. I need to watch a woman who is so many of the things I want to be—concert pianist, teacher, wife, mother. I need to know it's possible, to know I'm not going to have to choose career at the expense of family or family at the expense of career. I'm not really here to get Lilian Kallir's final word on Beethoven or Schumann. I just want to be near her, watch her perform, teach, walk, breathe, and laugh with her husband and daughter. She has such a musical laugh. I'm here to study the woman.

My mother and I are so different—I guess I've been turning to other women as role models for some time now. Still, I'm curious about my mother. There's so much I want to know—about what it was like to go to college when her mother never finished the eighth grade, what her childhood was like, what her dreams were. She can't really tell me. Says she doesn't remember much before the age of thirteen, when she had to move to Texas because of her asthma. I guess we have that in common—neither of us remembers her childhood. My mother doesn't remember mine, either.

Before I got to Aspen, I stopped in Denver to visit my grandfather, who was staying with my uncle and aunt. I asked Grandpa about Mom, what she was like as a little girl. His answers surprised me. He said she was mischievous. "Like the time she ran out into the street," he said. "She got spanked all right, then ran right back across the street and turned on the fire hydrant." My mother, mischievous? Maybe we were more alike than I thought. My aunt said my uncle used to brag so much about how smart and athletic my mother was that for a long time she didn't know he had any other brothers and sisters. She got straight A's in college chemistry, was number one in tennis. What made her give all that up? I wonder if I am my mother's cast-off dreams.

I want to go into this lesson prepared. At times, it feels like torture to make myself practice, to give myself wholly to it. At those times, I always feel that the hours spent practicing are hours that belong to someone else, but I'm not sure whom.

It was awkward with Sandi and Tom. I am connected with Sandi through my brother Paul, but he is the one thing we couldn't talk about. I wanted to talk about him so badly. I wanted to ask Sandi to drive with me to Cheyenne and visit his grave. But she is too excited about the new baby and her future with Tom to go visit the past. I don't blame her.

After seeing Sandi pregnant and so overjoyed about it, I wanted to give up music, go home, get pregnant, and never look back. But I know I'd look back, and I'd probably resent the child for the road I didn't take. Better to travel the road a bit further first.

The one time my brother's name came up we were standing at the top of Aspen Highlands looking across at the snow-covered peaks of the Maroon Bells and the valley hundreds of feet below.

I suppose the possibility of stepping off the edge brought us closer to Paul.

"We have to decide when to tell this child I was married before," Sandi patted her bulging tummy, "and that my husband died."

Is that all, I thought. Just that you were married before and he died? Nothing about the way you first saw his blue eyes and curly blond hair and heard his infectious laughter from across the university cafeteria? Nothing about how you wanted to be with the friends who crowded around him? Nothing else, not even his name? Will you tell this child my brother had any sisters?

I said nothing. I knew I was treading on thin ice. Before they were married Tom had asked Sandi to sever all ties with her dead husband's family. Sandi got rid of all of her photographs of Paul, his watch, his glasses, his clothes and books. They arrived at my house in a box. But she couldn't get rid of me. I made her promise. I'm so afraid of losing her. She's all I have left of my brother.

In the silence that followed, I took one step closer to the edge. Paul is dead. He left her, he left me. He left my brother, my sister, my parents. Why do I still want to join him?

Kallir has some good ideas on pedaling the third movement of the *Waldstein* Sonata. She's not as didactic as Shure is about Beethoven. She suggests I let the pedal up slightly after the first four of the ten measures, depending on the piano, the hall, and whether the acoustic is wet or dry. If it's dry I should hold the pedal all the way through. If there's lots of reverberation, I'll have to take a few half-pedals. I like her flexibility. I like the fact that it's based on having played the same piece on hundreds of pianos in hundreds of halls around the world.

I'm leaving Aspen early, so this is my last lesson. I'd be sadder, except Kallir invited me to study with her in New York.

It's easier to say good-bye when you know you'll see the person again.

We talk about repertoire, and my next recital program. I tell her I'm thinking of performing Bach's *Capriccio on the Departure of a Beloved Brother*. Why, she asks, with all the really great keyboard works of Bach, would I want to play that one?

I say I don't know.

Tomorrow I'm driving up to Cheyenne to visit my brother's grave. After six and a half years, I still can't think of anything to say except "fuck you" and "why?"

I wish I could just say good-bye.

AUGUST 1992, DENVER

My favorite group is art therapy. Trish hands out oil pastels, Conté crayons, charcoal, and huge sheets of gray paper. It's textured charcoal paper, the kind we used to reserve for final projects in my college life-drawing class.

"The idea in art therapy," Trish says, "is to draw what you can't yet talk about. Words will follow."

My first drawing is a black hole.

At the end of group, I sneak a box of pastels, some charcoal, and extra paper into my room.

My room faces west. From my bed I can see the mountains and watch the sky change colors at sunset. It's the one time of day I feel at home, no matter where I am. The sky is bigger here. It's hard to explain. You only know it if you've spent time out west.

There are Levolor blinds across my window, sealed between two panes of glass. Since the stripes are horizontal it feel less like a prison than it might. I can adjust the blinds, open or close them, but I can't pull them up out of the way. Blinds are sharps, and sharps are not allowed in a locked ward.

Just before sunset, light fills the room and creates a pattern of stripes across my desk and across the drawing paper. I like it. I draw the stripes, then start to draw Betty.

First I draw Betty in her red jumpsuit, waving. She is always cheerful. That's her downfall. Next, I draw Betty split in two, half red Betty, still waving, half white ghost. Then I draw the ghost whole, walking away, then floating out of the upper left-hand corner of the picture. At the bottom of the paper I write, "Betty goes bye-bye."

My mother's voice comes back, ten years ago like it's yesterday: "Unless you restore the warmth in your voice, I'm not going to talk to you on the phone." My mother and I wrote letters for a while, until I could put on Betty again.

Betty was the name of my mother's best friend in Cheyenne. She was hardly ever cheerful, but my mother talked to her all the time. I wanted my mother to talk to me the way she talked to her best friend, Betty.

Betty is my outer shell, a second skin. I am shedding her here. She's not really part of me inside. I don't lose control or consciousness when I'm putting on Betty. She's more like a piece of clothing I wear in public, a mask. For a long time people were fooled. My mother has always been fooled. Or maybe it's just that she can't really look at me until I've put on Betty, the way some people don't want to see you until you've showered, had a cup of coffee, and combed your hair in the morning.

In the second drawing I put Betty behind bars. I draw the horizontal shadows that stripe the paper, but leave an empty vertical space running down the center of the drawing. On the right side, half of Betty is waving from behind bars, her hand outlined in black. On the left side half a ghost is disappearing. At the bottom I write, "Betty waves good-bye."

In the third drawing Betty is still behind bars, but the vertical space that splits the drawing is now black. I've filled Betty in. She's still split in half, but whole. Nothing is missing now, just hidden behind a wall of black. The ghost half has a clear shape now—her white hand is on her white hip. The Betty hand is still outlined in black, but not waving. The third finger is extended. At the bottom I write, "Betty flips the bird."

I think about Schumann and the names he gave his divided self—Florestan and Eusebius. Florestan was named after the hero in the dungeon in Beethoven's *Fidelio*, who is chained to a rock, starving, and about to be killed. His wife, dressed up as a man, Fidelio, comes to rescue him. Florestan was Schumann's name for his outgoing, assertive side. Eusebius was named after a fourteenth-century priest who admired the Christian martyrs, and was himself persecuted and eventually executed. Eusebius was Schumann's name for his introverted, reflective side, probably his suicidal side, too. Schumann called Florestan and Eusebius his best friends. He claimed they cheered him up.

I don't think of Betty as a friend, or even as part of me. She is more like a shade I pull down so that no one can see in.

But Florestan and Eusebius are like windows into Schumann's soul, and he opens them for all to hear in his music. The first four of the eight *Fantasy Pieces* are a perfect balance of Schumann's twin selves: "In the Evening" (Eusebius) with its inwardly calm yet restless melody, and "Soaring" (Florestan) with its aggressive, almost violent 6/8 theme, are followed by the gentle questioning "Why?" (Eusebius), answered by "Whimsy" (Florestan), with its dancelike staccato chords in 3/4 time. The last four pieces are each combinations of Florestan and Eusebius, but still in perfect symmetry.

I see patients around me who call themselves all sorts of names, who answer by these names at various times, and I'm envious. They are at least themselves, or some part of themselves, at all times.

When I put on Betty, I am nobody. I am invisible. I need to get to know the parts of myself that I hide when I put on Betty, the parts that control me even when I'm wearing Betty like a coat.

Schumann once wrote to Clara Wieck, the celebrated pianist who later became his wife: "You want everything to be as though it's new and has never happened before, but there are old and eternal states that control us."

I look around me and what I see is a very old trick. Like Florestan's wife dressed up as a man to rescue her dying husband, you do what you have to do to survive, and to make sure others survive.

When life as who you are is unlivable, you must become someone else.

AUGUST–SEPTEMBER 1982, BOSTON

I'm working on a Haydn Sonata, E-flat major (Hob. XVI:49.) It's not the big one that begins with the rolled chord, the one most pianists play, it's the one just before that, the obscure one. I don't know why I didn't choose the more famous E-flat sonata. Was it the double thirds? I've handled double thirds in more difficult pieces. Chopin's Ballade in F Minor most recently. Actually, the difficult parts appeal to me. I can spin off most of the fast thirty-second-note runs at sight. Everything feels good under my fingers. Too good. Sensual even, which is why I didn't choose it.

It's not something I've talked to other pianists about, but there's a definite sensuality to touch at the piano. When my fingertips caress the keys, or brush them slightly, or even when they are dancing very quickly over arpeggios or scale passages, I have sensations I don't want to admit.

Sometimes at night, when Dan and I are falling asleep, I will flutter a trill on his leg, or grab a chord on his chest without realizing I'm touching him at all. It drives him crazy, but not in a good way. He's jealous of my music, almost as if I had another lover. Maybe I do.

Maybe I always have, and it's why I could never play music with the innocence of a child, even when I was a child. I suppose if you're somewhat precocious musically, and you're playing music that has an emotional depth beyond your experience, you feel things earlier than you're supposed to.

But the physicality is a problem. I've always played music that came naturally to me, at least physically. Emotionally, there has to be some kind of inner tension or conflict that I can connect to. Patricia Zander, my piano teacher in graduate school, wanted me to work on a piece of music that I couldn't automatically relate to, where I'd have to reach for the emotional connections. She didn't want me to get stuck, like an actor who could play only certain roles. She suggested Haydn.

The last time I'd played anything by Haydn, I was ten. I'd learned his Allegretto in A Major as part of a recital program. I was also learning the first movement of Beethoven's *Moonlight* Sonata that year. It was dark and melancholy, and somehow suited me better than Haydn. The Haydn felt like kid's stuff. It was full of arpeggios in triplets. I could whip them off easily. It was a happy little piece, and somewhat naive. There was a childlike innocence I didn't feel as a child. I remember the score, the etching of Papa Haydn on the front, my father's initials penciled in the upper right-hand corner.

That was the year we moved from Milwaukee to Cheyenne. I hated leaving my piano teacher, Miss Skinner, even though her gnarled fingers and musty old house used to scare me. I had no teacher for a while in Cheyenne, and was on the waiting list for Mrs. Thamer, the most prestigious piano teacher in town, who had a soft spot for ministers' kids and was willing to give them a discount on lessons. My father wanted to be sure I'd continue playing the piano, so he offered me twenty-five cents for every piece I worked on, then initialed it at the top after I played it for him. I don't know why music was so sacred in our house, but it was. Perhaps because my father's father loved music—he had an old player piano with music rolls ranging from Beethoven's *Emperor* Concerto to Scott Joplin's *Maple Leaf Rag*. My father himself had a huge record collection and I remember dancing around the living room to one of his favorite oldies—"well you blow through here, and the music goes round and round, whoa-oh-oh-oh-oh-oh, and it comes out here."

The piano was sacred, too. No one would touch me there. I was allowed to practice for hours. It reminds me of the Bible story about David playing his harp for King Saul and driving all of the evil demons out of him. My father was kinder while I played. I liked the idea of playing for money at first, but then it started to feel like he was buying each piece. I was afraid that one day he would own all of my music, so I stopped. I took the money, rode my bike to the music store, and bought the score for Beethoven's *Moonlight* Sonata.

Even without my father's initials at the top of the score, I still dislike Haydn. It's full of musical jokes I don't get. Patricia Zander suggested I listen to Mozart's opera, *The Magic Flute* (*Die Zauberflöte*), as a means of relating to the classical sense of humor. But even Papageno, the most comic figure in the opera, tries to hang himself. He sings for a long time while holding the rope, ties it to a tree, even drapes it around his neck, but he doesn't go through with it. If the rope had tightened, even by accident, it would have cut into his vocal cords. I suppose that would have been one way to end the aria, but it wouldn't have been funny. What makes this scene funny is that Papageno is singing about death, trying it on for size, but doesn't actually die.

The problem with Haydn's sense of humor is that there is never the remotest hint of death. I think he lived too long, wrote too many sonatas, trios, quartets, symphonies, and concertos. I prefer composers whose lives were snuffed out prematurely, like Mozart and Schubert, who had to make the most of too little time. Composers who considered ending their lives prematurely, like Beethoven, after he lost his hearing, or Schumann, who tried by jumping into the Rhine River, are also more interesting to me.

I like to think of music as a means of beating back time, making it expand or contract at will, making life feel longer than it actually is. Haydn's music makes me feel like I've got too much time on my hands, or in my hands, and for someone who's used to feeling that time is always about to run out, it's impossible.

In the Haydn sonata I'm working on now, at the very end of the slow movement, time runs down. This is the place that pulls me through the first two movements. Five measures from the end, there's a steady heartbeat of repeated eighth notes. In the last two measures the spaces between the eighth notes get longer and longer until there is only silence. It almost dies, but there are two more beats, two last breaths. The finale is a light-hearted minuet with frolicking triplets that lingers too long in E-flat major, but I suppose it's earned frivolity after the near death of the middle movement.

Since I got back from Aspen, my brother David's calls are more frequent, his voice desperately cheerful. He's been bringing up Baltimore, where we lived when we were little.

"I was Dad's slave," he says, and right away I remember Paul, David, and I, at nine, seven, and five, trudging up and down hundreds of stairs delivering Vacation Bible School pamphlets for our father. It was scary when people opened their doors, but sometimes when they'd invite us in, and give us Kool-Aid, I'd just want to stay and stay. I think about the hair we had then—my blonde curls, my brothers' crew cuts. Paul was blond with blue eyes, always squinting into the sun, David had brown hair and brown eyes, and one eye wandered. When David was three, he had surgery on the eye that wandered, but it didn't work. His eye still wandered, and he never quite got over the surgery. When I was given my very first doll, with eyes that opened and closed, David took both eyes out, then proudly displayed her, saying, "See, I fixed her. Now both eyes are the same."

When David talks about the way Dad used to beat him, the way Dad would shave his head as punishment, he is laughing the whole time. My stomach hurts. I know David hated getting his hair buzzed off. He was always vain about his hair, still is.

When David comes back to the present—tells me how quickly his new Toyota Celica accelerates up to ninety miles per hour, how he's been cutting corners close at high speeds, and how he almost spun off the road the other day, I'm scared.

"I think you should go see a therapist," I say.

He laughs.

"No, I mean it."

I keep telling my parents he needs help, but they say my therapist is putting ideas into my head. It's a conspiracy, they say. It's the way therapists make their money.

I tell my own therapist I'm worried, that David is starting to have car accidents again. She says I have reason to worry. After all, it's the way Paul used to talk.

I remember the year before Paul died, David ran a red light at a four-way intersection and hit three other cars. He almost lost his eye—the one that wanders. He'd made it back safe from Vietnam. It was the war inside that was killing him.

My therapist doesn't believe in accidents. Her sister died in a car accident, only she doesn't believe it was an accident. If she's putting ideas into my head that weren't there before, it's only that the next time David has an accident, he could die. It wouldn't matter whether it was his fault or another driver's. Dead is dead.

Dan and I are leaving for Vermont soon. A ten-day bike trip. I'm thinking of canceling, of flying down to Florida to see David. His wife, Vickie, is there with him now, and their son, little Dave. He keeps asking me when we're coming.

But Dan really needs this vacation. He's sick of my music, sick of my family, and ready for a break. I can't back out on him now. Besides, he gave me a new Peugeot twelve-speed for my birthday. It's light. It's fast. I owe him this trip.

Still, I'm afraid to be on my bike for ten days straight. Three weeks before I played in Symphony Hall I was speeding down the bike path along the Charles River and hit a ditch where a piece of asphalt was missing. I flew over the handlebars and hit my head. It was dark for a long time. When I opened my eyes I was inside an ambulance. I asked for my bike.

"Just be glad you're alive, lady," the attendant said. "That helmet saved your life."

My parents bought me the helmet for my birthday. My mother says I've always been accident-prone.

It's only the fourth day of vacation, Dan says, and we blew the budget on music. Tanglewood. I say we blew it on dinner. The

Red Lion Inn. He says food is necessary, music is not. I say music is food. More and more, music is the thing that's between us. When I married Dan I thought he loved music as much as I did. After all, he'd grown up with two Steinways in the dining room, Bach, Brahms, and Beethoven filling the house. Is that what we're fighting over—music in the dining room instead of food?

Tanglewood is like no other place I know. Tall majestic pine trees tower over a rolling green carpet of grass. Just over the hedge near Lion's Gate you can see down into the Stockbridge Bowl. It sparkles like blue ice. We canoed there a few days ago, before the concert. It was so quiet, so peaceful, the only sound you could hear was Dan's paddle dipping into the water. He's an expert with a canoe. No fight over that.

After fighting over whether to go to the concert, we fought over where to sit. Dan wanted to sit outside on the lawn—the tickets are cheaper and you can look up at the stars. I love stargazing, but I can't stand the noisy picnicking crowd. They spread out linen tablecloths with candelabras and squeaky lawn chairs and talk and eat through the entire concert. Why can't they eat before the concert? I wanted to be inside the shed where you can really hear the music. Dan gave in. We heard Ken Noda perform Mozart's Piano Concerto in A Major with the Boston Symphony Orchestra, Seiji Ozawa conducting. The playing was so exuberant, so animated, I found myself waiting until the end of each long phrase to breathe. I decided to learn the A-major concerto.

Life is short. Why waste time on Haydn when there is so much Mozart?

We spent last night at Molly Stark Campground near Bennington, Vermont. Since we're biking from inn to inn and we've blown our budget, I suggested we camp out. We hadn't slept in a tent since the early days of our marriage when we used to backpack in the Rockies and the Cascades, and I thought it might be romantic.

It wasn't. Even if it had been romantic, what can you do in separate sleeping bags? Toss and turn and sweat, that's what. I slept on a rock, which I didn't feel for some reason until I woke up screaming "No, no, no!" In my dream, someone had been digging fingernails into my back.

The dream went like this: I'm swimming in a huge pool the size of a warehouse, when I hear a woman screaming for help. I swim over to the middle of the pool. The woman is drowning in a bathtub full of boiling water. Mar, my best friend from college, is standing by watching.

"Why aren't you helping her?" I ask.

"She tried to kill me, and I'm just going to let her die."

I pull the woman out of the water. She is limp in my arms, almost dead. Then her eyelids start to flutter. I support her head and back, the way you'd hold a baby. She grabs me and digs her fingernails into my neck. I carry her toward the edge of the pool, and the closer we get to safety, the more she digs her fingernails into my back. The pain is excruciating. I feel a trickle of blood down my neck and cry out. As I walk past other people in the pool they turn their heads away. Nearer the edge, I see men in white coats waiting to take the woman off my hands. She digs her fingers into the cuts in my neck and begs me not to let her go. I know she is dying, that I can't help her, and that if I keep carrying her she will eventually kill me. But the closer we get to the men in white, the more she screams. I pause near the edge of the pool before letting her go, then cry when they take her out of my arms. I feel sorry for the woman, but I can't handle her. "How could you?" she screams. "How *could* you?" I cover my face with my hands the way I always have when my mother says those three words.

Dan held me through two sleeping bags until I stopped shaking and fell asleep again.

I had another dream, this time about my father. It's scary. He is naked and coming on to me sexually. I've blocked a lot of the details—it makes me feel sick. When I think about my father when I was little, pulling my pants down, pulling my brothers' pants down, making us watch as he pulled the belt out of his own pants, I think something was very wrong with that. Still, I've always wanted to be closer to him. My therapist says little girls often have sexual fantasies about their fathers. Is this a fantasy or a nightmare? It's a dream that makes me want to wash.

I wake up sliding out of the tent, sleeping bag and all. When I open my eyes and see Dan clenching the bottom of my bag, I feel like a cavewoman who's just been dragged out into the light.

"Up 'n' at 'em!" Dan says, dropping my sleeping bag.

"Ouch! Those are my feet."

"C'mon, let's go. Seven miles to breakfast."

What is it about morning that makes some people pop out of bed like a piece of toast and others drag around like they've been run over by an eighteen-wheeler? My head is throbbing. I see lights with my eyes closed or open, but open is worse. I know I'll throw up at least once by the end of the day.

Dan pulls up the rainfly, is about to collapse the tent.

"Hey, wait—how am I supposed to get dressed?"

"In your bag."

I hear Dan pulling up stakes. I see our bikes already loaded up with panniers and roll packs, leaning against a tree. My light-as-a-feather Peugeot looks dwarfed under its load. I look more closely and see that my back tire is perfectly flat.

"We've got trouble." I point to my tire.

Dan runs over to the bikes. "Damn!"

I worm my way back into what's left of the tent, rub my temples, and try to block out the nightmares, the worst I've had in years. I take out my notebook, the one I keep next to me at the piano to collect my thoughts. Distraction at the piano can cost me a few measures, sometimes a whole page. But once I commit thoughts to pen and paper, my mind is clear and I can focus again. I hope it works now. Distraction on my bike could cost a lot more.

The tent collapses on top of me.

"Hey!"

"What are you doing in there?"

"Getting dressed."

"Hurry up—we've lost half the morning."

The bad half, I hope. I jam my pen into the metal spiral back of my notebook, then shove it into the bottom of my sleeping bag.

Dan has fixed the flat, taken the panniers off the back of my bike and loaded everything onto the back of his. The car is safely parked at the ranger's station and we are heading down the road out of Molly Stark Campground to begin our seven-day trek through the hills of Vermont. Dan is just ahead of me, running his bike down the hill. He's ecstatic, like a ten-year-old boy, and throws himself onto his bike with the grace of a ballet dancer. We are finally on our way. Maybe this trip will pull us closer together again. There's nothing we both love more than biking. The cool morning air stings my face awake. Seven miles to Hogback Ski Area and breakfast.

Bang.

Dan's rear tire.

Five flats between Bennington and Manchester, a slow leak and a bulging tube up the hill out of Manchester, and two dragging, deflated spirits. We gave up biking from inn to inn after arriving exhausted at the 1811 House in Manchester and discovering that we had to bike another five miles to dinner because the English couple who'd just bought the place hadn't finished renovating the kitchen.

The next morning, Dan surprised me with breakfast in bed. A blue and white English china tea set, with eggs, bacon, and toast on a silver tray. He must have helped the innkeepers figure out how to use their unfinished kitchen. I was grateful, especially since we didn't have to ride to breakfast.

Instead, we took the River Road and old Route 7 back to Bennington to pick up the car. We rode past farm houses, a little red school house, through a covered bridge and into a poorer part of Vermont—trailers with yards full of engine parts and rusted-out antique iron bedsteads—and finally past an old stone water mill converted into a house on the outskirts of Bennington. That was the best ride we had the whole week—no flats. It was as if once we'd given up trying and waved the white flag, the road was all ours.

By the time we reached Bennington, I was feeling like a nomad, wandering aimlessly around Vermont. My notebook as dreamkeeper had failed me. I couldn't stop thinking about the men in white coats. And I was worried about my brother David—tried to call him from several places on the road, but got no answer.

Home is disappearing again.

We drove to Bridgewater Corners this morning. Last stop, October Country Inn. It's a little red house backed up to a hill. An old wooden swing hangs from the side porch. It's nostalgic, but I'm sick of nostalgia. Until I walk into the living room and see a baby grand, an old Sohmer, near the window. I drop my bags, sit down, and play a few notes. It's out of tune, but who cares? After seven days on the road and five flat tires, I'm home.

Five flats. My hands reach for G-flat and D-flat, and I'm playing "Evening," the first of Schumann's *Fantasy Pieces*. The right hand melody is like balm, and the left hand triplets soothe me like a mother rocking a child to sleep. D-flat major: five flats. I laugh, then skip to the third piece, "Why?" then to "Whims" and the middle section of "Dream Visions," all in D-flat major. It's a game now. I try and remember every piece I've ever played in five flats.

Chopin, B-flat minor Nocturne. I play the melancholy opening line, struggle through the eleven against six, then twenty-two against twelve, remembering why I've never performed this piece in public. I could never get the right hand to fit the left without leaving gaps or bunching the notes together. I can't remember the second page, so I skip to the middle section in D-flat major, *pianissimo* with descending thirds, fifths, and sixths. It sounds like distant horn calls.

I think of my brother David practicing his trumpet from behind closed doors. Sometimes while I was practicing, he'd stride into the living room with a score in one hand and his trumpet in the other and flop his music open in front of mine. We always played the same duet over and over again. "The Secret," in B-flat. I'd play the accompaniment faster and faster until David would finally laugh into his mouthpiece and have to stop. He'd take another breath, lift his trumpet to his lips, and we'd be off again. I wonder what he did with that old trumpet. He quit playing when he left home.

Scriabin, B-flat minor Prelude. It's spooky in the beginning, hushed, like someone is sneaking into your room late at night. I play the sixteenth note triplet upbeat as *sotto voce* and *misterioso* as possible. The right hand melody sounds like the "Funeral March" from Chopin's B-flat minor Sonata, except Scriabin throws in an extra beat every other measure, 5/8 alternating with 4/8. The constant rhythmic change builds so much tension you feel like the music might burst before it reaches *fortissimo*. This is the only piece more terrifying to me than Schumann's *In the Night*. Why am I so drawn to terror?

Scriabin's Fifteenth Prelude, op. 11 in D-flat major.

I know it intimately, too intimately, in fact. My left hand starts the slow double thirds, reaches for the top voice in the thumb. The first full phrase is for the left hand alone. I try to make it sing. There's a knot in my stomach, but I keep going anyway, adding the simple right hand melody. I remember the day I learned this piece. I was sitting at the old rosewood piano in Dan's parents' house—the Steinway seven-foot B near the French doors in the dining room, the one with the autographs of famous pianists written inside: Claudio Arrau, Grant Johannesen, Artur Rubinstein. Dan had just pulled out of the driveway, his desert-gray Volvo loaded down with ski equipment, fall and winter clothes. He'd postponed his senior year of college and was driving to Vail, Colorado, to race and teach skiing. After waving good-bye, I walked back into the house with Dan's mother, sat down at the piano, and learned this Scriabin Prelude to console myself. It's stayed with me, and whenever I'm saying good-bye to someone I love, I play that piece.

Just as I am about to resolve the last chord, a man strolls into the living room. Please don't talk to me, I think, A-flat major chord vibrating, waiting to go home to D-flat. The man sits down next to me on the bench.

"Hi, I'm Eliot," he says loudly. The A-flat chord has dissipated. "Sounds nice, but do you know anything light, you know, Broadway or something?"

I look into the man's eyes. They are dark brown, round and intense. He smiles broadly through his beard, like he's been smiling every day of his life. He's annoying, but handsome. If it weren't for the constant smile, I'd say he looked like my brother David.

"Sure, I know some Broadway."

I switch to E-flat and play Sondheim's "Send in the Clowns."

The men in white coats came; they took my brother David away. The information came to me in pieces over the phone. David thought he was Jesus at the Last Supper. The end of the world is coming, he said. Armageddon, a nuclear holocaust.

Tommy, his friend from the power plant, signed the papers. You could say Tommy was Judas, only he didn't kiss my brother's cheek or hang himself, and nothing else went the way it did in the Bible.

David says our brother Paul is still alive. I want to believe him. Maybe he rose from the dead.

Before he thought he was Jesus, David checked into a Holiday Inn. In his Bible he'd written, "The Holy Spirit has entered me. My life is going to be changed from this day forward." On the third day he checked out, burned all his credit cards, threatened to kill his wife and son, and kissed his wife's little sister on the lips. It was more than a kiss, she said, a lot more.

The call came after five days of silence from my family, the five days since David was taken to a private psychiatric hospital in West Palm Beach. I'd been practicing Liszt, the sixth Paganini Etude. My right arm hurt from practicing the octaves in the seventh variation too fast.

I took in my mother's words with huge gulps of air, then held my breath for the final blow: "Your brother bought a gun."

II. AUGUST 1992/
OCTOBER 1982

AUGUST 1992, DENVER

"THE HOLE IN THE MIND."

Nancy Coles, the clinical director of the center, is giving a lecture on trauma theory. She draws a black hole on the board. I can't take my eyes off her stomach. She is huge with child.

"This is the traumatic event." She points to the black hole. "It's intrusive, unpredictable, creates a state of helplessness, and disrupts homeostasis. Trauma affects everything— even one's balance. Many people who've been traumatized walk on the outsides of their shoes."

I think of my father, how bow-legged he was, how he wore down the outside soles of his shoes. What traumatized him? The war? He fought in the Battle of the Bulge, a sergeant in Patton's Third Army. Is that what made him violent? I am looking and looking for some way to preserve the good father, to forgive the bad one.

"In order to preserve homeostasis, one must be able to screen out certain stimuli." She draws an arching dotted line, like an eyebrow over the black hole. "People who've been chronically traumatized are unable to screen out certain noises, movements, smells, and sights. The stimulus barrier has holes." She draws smaller arches like umbrellas over the spaces between the lines. "These are the defenses people develop to ward off the trauma. People will do almost anything to avoid the hole in their minds. You need to find a safe place before you can look into the hole."

Later, I draw Betty's ghost with a white chalk line that looks like Morse code. It's the kind of line we traced when we learned to draw circles in kindergarten. I always drew outside the line to show that I could draw a circle by myself.

Inside the white chalk line, I draw a black charcoal outline, half dots and dashes, the other half solid line. And inside that line I draw Betty, only I'm not sure it's Betty since the red is gone, and nobody's waving. She's half-black, half-white. The black half is holding a knife, the white half has her hand on her hip. If you pretend the drawing is a maze, there is always a way through the dots and dashes to the center, where the navel should be. The black hole.

Now that the red is gone from my drawings, I know Betty is dead. She was the cover. Now anyone can see through the dotted line. What's left is the black hole. It's the same black hole I drew the first day I came here, only it's not the hole in my mind. It's the hole in my belly, the one that was left when they cut the cord, and anyone who wasn't my mother could feed me.

Back in my room, I open my closet and examine the soles of all of my shoes. If anything, it's the inside soles that are worn down, especially under the big toe.

Maybe I don't belong here.

"Do you have a safe place?" Doug asks.

I can't answer. My teeth are chattering. I'm shivering. I shake my head no, hug my arms tightly around me. What is happening to me? We are sitting outside in the courtyard. It's eighty-five degrees, at least. Why am I shivering? Why can't I talk? Do something, I think, get me out of this body.

"I'm going to count from five to one," Doug says, "and I want you to go to your safe place."

What safe place? What is he talking about? I thought this place was supposed to be safe. There are enough locked doors and high brick walls to keep out an army.

"Five—"

Four, three, two, one, zero, blast-off. I want to be out of here on a rocket, but no, my teeth are still clicking together like castanets and I'm shivering out of control. I don't know what's worse, to feel this out of control and be watching from the inside, or to blast off like a rocket, disappear completely. I can't seem to leave my body no matter how hard I try.

"Four, I want you to start breathing deeply—"

I take a breath, let it out.

"Three, that's good, take another breath—"

I chatter in triplets now, every few measures a breath.

"Good, you're moving into that safe place—"

Diminuendo, ritardando, a staccato exhale with rests, a sob.

"Two, you're almost there—"

I open my mouth, inhale.

"One. You're safe. Now close."

I exhale, close my mouth, begin breathing through my nose. Is this what it means to be safe? I want to marry Doug, have him count from five to one every night for the rest of my life.

"I'm going to teach you to count," Doug says.

I am standing in front of the bathroom mirror, washing my face. I have just thrown up for the seventh time this week. Once a day keeps the bad thoughts away. More than once might be pushing it. I've lost twelve pounds in two weeks. If I lose any more, I'm going to have my privileges yanked.

Today I was supposed to go to "Eating Issues" with Cheryl. I don't have eating issues, I protest. I eat everything on my plate. I just can't keep it down.

Dr. Grant, my shrink, asks me what I am feeling about my mother. It's supposed to relate to food. Nothing, I tell her. It's that blind woman I can't stand. My mother used to say "think of others worse off than yourself," and it always worked. It gets my mind right off my own problems. So now there's Alice, who's just been admitted. She has a seeing eye dog for a roommate, but I've been elected to lead her around from group to group and show her what's what. I tell Dr. Grant she reminds me of my mother.

"Is your mother blind?"

"Selective blindness," I say.

But that's not why Alice reminds me of my mother. It's her helplessness. She needs me, and I am there for her, because I am the strong one. This is what I tell myself. After all, I can see, and she can't. So last night, I led Alice into the lounge and my friend, Sue, suggested Scrabble. I am the undisputed Scrabble champion here, and it's one of the few areas of my life where I have any self-esteem intact. But I have never thrown a game, and I was not about to play Scrabble with a blind woman. I shook my head desperately and mouthed "not with Alice," but it was too late. Alice said she'd love to play.

Sue and I looked at each other and shrugged. Alice, sensing our discomfort, said, "I just need someone to tell me what letters I have and what gets played where." Sue volunteered. Alice drew seven letters from the bag (you're not supposed to look anyway) and let Sue arrange them on the little wooden tray. I drew my seven. We played three or four turns, respectable moves in the twenties and thirties, Sue describing the board to Alice, and Alice whispering to Sue which tiles to put where. I was ahead, but not by much, and was kind of relishing having the upper hand after being Alice's servant all week. Still, I opened up the triple. I mean, how good can it feel to beat a blind woman at Scrabble? I was thinking about this when I heard Alice whisper her play to Sue. I wasn't surprised when Sue laid down Alice's B in front of "lasted," or went down the left-hand side of the board with the E, or the A or the R, landing on the triple. But after adding -ing, Sue let out a "Yes!" and Alice counted on her fingers. Bingo on a triple. Eighty-seven points.

That's what reminds me of my mother, I tell Dr. Grant. Whenever we played Ping-Pong or tennis, Mom would complain about how tired or out of breath she was, how I was so much younger and stronger, and I would start to feel bad. Then she would nail me with a stroke to the back of the court.

Dr. Grant suggests I stop taking care of Alice and focus on my own feelings, and see if that helps me keep down dinner.

After therapy, I'm lying on my bed thinking of Alice. I think of how all those times she was raped as a kid she couldn't see who did it, and how much worse off she is than I am. I close my eyes and try to imagine what it's like not to see, but what I see are blue and orange stripes. I open my eyes and I see the light coming under the door. I close my eyes and see orange and blue stripes again, on seersucker cotton.

Suddenly I don't feel sorry for Alice anymore. I start to envy her. I start to feel pissed off at her for getting me to wait on her hand and foot all week, and then beating me at Scrabble. I think of how she could remember the board, where every tile had been placed, not ever missing a move. But she could see because Sue was telling her what was there, not because she really saw. I wonder if it's worse to see and be told that what you see is not there.

Alice can open her eyes or close them, but no matter what else happens, she will never, ever have to look at her father's pajamas.

OCTOBER 1982, NEW YORK

I'm taking the shuttle to La Guardia. It's my first lesson with Lilian Kallir since Aspen. I'm chasing my dreams on a plane to New York while my brother loses his mind in a mental hospital in West Palm Beach. Hardly seems fair.

David's been in the hospital almost two weeks. His dreams get more elusive by the day. In August, he'd told me what they were: He was going to finish college, take the LSATs, and go to law school. Neither Dad nor Mom wanted him to become a lawyer. Dad let him know in no uncertain terms. "Lawyers are the scum of the earth," he said.

"I'd like to finish law school and fling the degree in Dad's face," David told me.

I told him he'd make a great lawyer. "But first," I pleaded, "could you go see a therapist?"

As a kid, David was the runt. Always making trouble to prove himself, I guess. But in high school, when he shot up to six foot four, towering over the rest of the family, he was the star. Captain of the debating team, National Merit Scholar, first trumpet in the all-state band. He had enough trophies in speech and debate to cover his entire dresser top. Dusted them off once a week. He graduated with honors, and a full scholarship to Northwestern in Chicago. But the night of graduation he got stoned and totaled his car. Instead of going to college, he signed up for the Navy, and Vietnam. The first thing they did in boot camp was shave his head. His hair was his pride and joy. It must have killed him to lose it.

How many paranoid schizophrenics get to be lawyers? Dr. Kaye, my brother's psychiatrist, thinks that's what's wrong with him. David sees things in groups of threes and fours. "Look, there are four of us in the room," he says, when it's only David and Dr. Kaye. That's what the doctor told Vickie.

Maybe there *were* four in the room just then. David could have been seeing the four of us, as kids. That's what I think of when I think of four. It's probably why I love string quartets. Four playing in harmony.

But now we are three. Paul is dead. David doesn't believe that right now, but then maybe he does, and he's going back and forth about it in his mind. Sometimes we are four. Sometimes we are three.

When I think groups of three, I think three out of four Saturdays a month, three out of the four of us got the belt. I don't think my sister, Karen, got the belt—she was the baby, and we all protected her. I didn't get it as often as my brothers. I don't remember if it was less than three or more than four times a month. Still, the fact that David sees things in threes and fours is no reason to call him a paranoid schizophrenic.

But David is talking about head shavings, and that was more like two out of four. Only the boys got their heads shaved when we lived in Baltimore, and sometimes only David. That's what he's been telling Dr. Kaye about. Mom says he hated getting his head shaved. "He was so humiliated." She said it like she felt bad for him.

It's funny, the things that stay in your mind and the things that go. David remembers the head shaving, but I don't. My mother remembers it, too, but there's so much she doesn't remember. I wonder why David got his head shaved but I didn't. I must have escaped because my father loved my blonde curls. "You were such a cute little blonde girl," he always said. Then my hair got dark.

Both of my brothers had crew cuts, but back then that was the style. Maybe it was the *way* Dad shaved David's head that was hard. There was always a kind of power in hair in our family, and my father was starting to lose his when he shaved my brothers' heads. It reminds me of Aslan, the lion in C. S. Lewis's *The Lion, the Witch, and the Wardrobe*. Before the witch was about to kill Aslan, she ordered an ogre to shave off his mane. "Snip, snip, snip, went the shears." I'll never forget that part. "He's only a great cat after all," the ogre cried after he'd shaved Aslan's mane.

They tied Aslan down with ropes. I wonder how my father kept David still in the chair long enough to shave his head. He was only a little boy, but he could kick hard. I imagine David struggling to get out of that chair, and suddenly I have to move from my seat. I undo my seat belt, excuse myself to the guy sitting in the aisle seat, and make it to the bathroom at the back of the plane just in time. Once the door is locked, and the fan is running, my chest starts to heave.

Twenty minutes later, after I've splashed cold water over it, my face is still blotchy and red. When I come back to my seat, I try to ignore the man I have to climb over. He looks lost in the sports section of *the New York Times*. Probably some businessman living vicariously through the Yankees. It's a good thing he's reading, because I'm going to have to start practicing soon, and on a plane it can be slightly embarrassing.

I take out my Beethoven sonatas, flip through to the *Waldstein*, and start thumping out the opening repeated chords on the tray table. Luckily, there's no one sitting in front of me. Sometimes the vibration goes right through the seat back and I get a dirty look from the passenger sitting there and have to stop. Today, I can't afford to. I didn't get to warm up this morning before I left, and this is my only chance.

I'm thumping out the end of the exposition, when out of my peripheral vision, I see the newspaper go down in the guy's lap. He could be folding a page over, or he could be stopping. I hope he doesn't ask me what I'm doing, or make some joke about how it would probably sound better on a piano. Now I'm practicing the harmonic changes in the development, which is where I'm most likely to have a memory slip. I'm playing the whole sonata for Kallir today, and I don't want to screw up. The man folds the sports section in half and looks over at my music. Please, please, don't talk to me.

"What are you working on?" he asks.

"Music," I say, hoping that if I keep on playing, he'll leave me alone.

"What music?"

Oh, God, here it comes, some stupid joke. I'm going to have to stop.

"Beethoven."

He leans over to look more closely at the music, just brushing my left arm. He probably wants me to think he can read notes as well as he can read the newspaper.

"Ah, the *Waldstein*," he says, "hard piece." This time he picks up the arts section of the *Times*.

I go back to the development again, but now I'm distracted. He must be a pianist. How else could he tell from the middle of the first movement that it's the *Waldstein*? I flip back to the opening—op. 53, it says. No hint there. I wonder if he's a professional or amateur musician. I lean over and tap him lightly on the shoulder.

"Excuse me, but are you a pianist?"

"No, I'm a violist."

Definitely a professional. No amateur violist would recognize the *Waldstein* at sight.

"Oh."

"You, however, must be a pianist."

He's teasing me, but I sort of like it. He has nice eyes, kind of a twinkle, and an impish grin.

"Right."

Why can't I think of something witty to say?

"How about those Yankees?" I say, regretting it almost immediately since I don't know whether they're winning or losing. I'm not even sure that's what he was reading about.

"They're finished for the season."

"Oh, that's too bad." Oh brother. I wish I knew baseball as well as he knows Beethoven. "Where do you play?"

"Baseball or viola?"

"Viola." I laugh. The guy has a sense of humor.

"I live in New York, but I travel a lot. I play in a string quartet."

"Really? What's your name?"

"Michael Tree, yours?"

I tell him my name. He shakes my hand. Tree. Michael Tree. I know that name from somewhere.

"Juilliard Quartet?"

"Guess again."

"Guarneri?"

"Right."

Oh God, I am sitting next to Michael Tree, the violist from the Guarneri String Quartet. My face is tingling, like it's been poked with thousands of tiny needles. I am so hot. I must be fire engine red by now.

"I can't believe it. I've worn out your recordings of the Beethoven Quartets. I've seen your picture a thousand times. I'm so embarrassed." I stick out my hand.

"We already shook hands, remember?" He laughs. "Where are you performing the *Waldstein?*"

"I'm not really performing—I have a lesson with Lilian Kallir."

"Ah, Lilian. Wonderful pianist." The flight attendant announces our descent, orders us to put seats and tray tables in the upright position.

"You know, we're going right by Lilian and Claude's apartment—would you like to share a cab?"

"We?"

"Well, yes, my colleagues and I." Michael points to the seat across from me. I look over and there is Arnold Steinhardt, the Guarneri Quartet's first violinist, his lanky legs spread out in the aisle.

We take two cabs, since there isn't room for all the instruments and five people. Arnold is in the front seat of our cab. I ride with Michael in the back seat, hold my breath most of the way, hang on to every word of the conversation. They are playing a concert in Boston soon and Michael offers me free tickets. When we pull up in front of Kallir's building on West Eighty-ninth, I say thank you about twenty times.

"Say hello to Lilian for us," Michael says, "and don't worry about the *Waldstein*—it sounded pretty good on the plane."

On the shuttle back to Boston, I am rereading Maynard Solomon's *Beethoven*, a biography with a psychoanalytic slant.

I'm wondering if I'll be teaching the "Life and Works of Beethoven" course again. It's not clear whether enrollments will be high enough. Still, I'd better prepare the first lecture.

"In the fantasy which Freud and Otto Rank named the 'Family Romance', the child replaces one or both of his parents with elevated surrogates," Solomon writes.

I see these words, underlined in pencil, and I wonder if this is why my lesson with Kallir was a disappointment. She was excited about my performance of the *Waldstein*, and sent me off with encouraging words. "Keep up the good work," she said. Why was I so disappointed, then, when I left?

Solomon zeroes in on a curious fact of Beethoven's life— that he allowed rumors to circulate undisputed that he was the illegitimate son of Frederick the Great, king of Prussia. Beethoven's father, Johann, a music teacher and an alcoholic who beat his son regularly and sometimes shut him up in the cellar, was certainly worth replacing. Unlike Mozart's father, who encouraged his son's prodigious improvisation, Beethoven's father quickly silenced his first attempts: "Once he was playing without notes; his father happened in and said: 'What silly trash are you scraping away at now? Scrape according to the notes; otherwise your scraping won't be of much use.'"

My own father's words echo in my ears. During a visit over a year ago, a wealthy parishioner from his church invited me to perform a recital in his home. I was practicing the

Schumann Fantasy in my father's house when he wandered into the living room. "What are you practicing for?" he said. "No one will listen to you anyway." Later that day, the man who invited me to perform wiped his eyes when I finished. I thanked him for listening, and returned to my father's house, not knowing whose ears to believe, not knowing if I'd humiliated my father or made him proud.

I was confused, especially since my father was the one who had bought me the piano when I was six. I'd begged for a piano so I could practice at home instead of at the church. My parents could barely afford the payments, and I had the feeling everyone in the family resented me for it. Later, there were all those times my father took me into piano stores and had me sit down at a grand and play for the salesman. I was his little Paderewski, he said, pronouncing it "Paderooski" so many times that it took me a while to connect the name to a real pianist, a dead pianist, whose name appeared on all of my Chopin editions. My father offered to buy me the grand piano if I won this competition or that. I'd win the competition, but never the piano. He was always upping the ante. At age sixteen, I decided to quit. My father laid down the law—as long as I was living under his roof, he said, I had to play. I ran away from home. I washed dishes for a couple of weeks at a summer camp in southern Colorado. My brother David showed up, packed me into his blue VW, and played the Beatles' "She's Leaving Home" on his eight-track the whole ride back. Once I was home again, I started practicing and haven't stopped since.

So now that I'm not living under my father's roof, and I'm making something of myself—the beginnings of a concert career, a university teaching job—he asks me why I'm still practicing.

I'm not sure anyone can ever quell my uncertainty about making music—none of the surrogate mothers or fathers who have taken me under their loving wings—not Lilian Kallir nor Claude Frank, not my mother-in-law, not even Beethoven himself, were he to return from the dead and tell me he approved of my playing of his Sonata in C, op. 53.

The pilot announces we're free to move about the cabin. I drop my tray table, take out my notebook, and reopen Solomon's *Beethoven* to another underlined passage. It is the text of what may have been Beethoven's first song, *To an Infant (An einen Säugling)*, composed when he was twelve. I jot down the words at the top of my lecture notes, under "family background." If I teach the course, I'll begin with this early song: "You still do not know whose child you are . . ."

I think of Beethoven as a twelve-year-old, wondering who his real parents were. How he eventually chose his grandfather Ludwig, the esteemed *Kapellmeister*, and a musician of far greater talent than Beethoven's father. Apparently, Beethoven's grandfather did not approve of his son Johann's marriage to Beethoven's mother, Maria Magdalena. Yet she eventually teamed up with her father-in-law against her alcoholic husband, and encouraged her young son to emulate his grandfather instead of his father.

I've had so many surrogate parents over the years. It started in Milwaukee with Miss Skinner, a stern but kind piano teacher with gnarled arthritic hands, and continued with Mrs. Thamer, my piano teacher in Cheyenne, then parents of various friends from grade school all the way through college, when my piano teacher became my mother-in-law. I gained a kind and gentle father-in-law, too, and grandparents-in-law who adored me. So in marrying Dan, I quite happily gained a whole new family. In college, I had three sets of surrogate parents I could count on—Liz and Dick Cole, who were my best friend Marilyn's parents; Harry and Marj Dixon, a professor and his wife who took me to Europe, and eventually took me into their home; and Mil and Fil, my parents-in-law. My friend, Mar, used to give me a hard time about it. "How many parents do you need?" she'd say, laughing.

When my brother Paul hanged himself, I got the news in Harry Dixon's study. Marj was there, Mar had come home with me. Mar's parents and Dan's parents came over that evening. Dan was already in Vail. His parents offered to fly me to Cheyenne for the funeral. My own parents didn't want me to come. "Since it's already December," they said, "why don't you finish out the semester and come home for Christmas?" I couldn't do that. I had to see my brother again, even if it was only to look at him inside the coffin. Mar stayed with me, held me through the night. I woke up screaming "No!" trying to get the image of my brother, suspended from a rope, out of my head. Asleep and awake I had nightmares. After that, Mar never asked how many parents I needed.

Now I wish David had gone to the funeral. Maybe he wouldn't be in a mental hospital right now, thinking Paul is alive.

The flight attendant arrives with the drink tray, which always seems like a big ordeal on such a short flight. I order a Bloody Mary without the vodka, and read on in Solomon.

In 1812, Beethoven copied Telemachus's words to Athena into his diary: "My mother saith that he is my father; for myself I know it not, for no man knoweth who hath begotten him."

Beethoven took this statement quite seriously. For most of his life, he refused to accept that his baptismal certificate, listing his parentage and date of birth, was accurate. He apparently had an older brother, Ludwig Maria, who'd died at birth. He claimed the certificate belonged to that older brother, leaving the question of his own parentage open.

There have been so many times I've wanted different parents, or at least additional ones, but I've never wondered who my real parents were. I look too much like my father to be mistaken for anyone else's daughter, but I don't look much like my mother. At least she's always told me so—"You're your father's daughter," she'd say, "you look like him, not me."

Whenever she said that her voice was like ice, smooth and wet, too cold to touch. I never knew what I did to make me his, not hers.

Still, last year I wondered if I really belonged to either of them. I was riding in my parents' car from Green Bay, Wisconsin, where they and my sister, Karen, lived, to Milwaukee, where we were having a family reunion with my father's relatives. Dan was following us in our Volvo, which we'd driven from Boston. I sat in the front seat with my father, at my mother's request. For as long as I can remember I was asked to sit in the front with my father. On long car trips when we'd drive all night, I was the one who would keep him awake at the wheel, patting his thighs with my small hands as if I were playing the piano, singing to him, whatever it took. But my privileged position always felt wrong somehow, drove another wedge between my mother and me.

We were late leaving for the reunion, and Dad was ranting and raving about Wisconsin drivers being the worst in the nation. He went on and on, raising his fist at the other drivers, who as far as I could tell were minding the speed limit. I reminded him that he'd said that about the drivers in every state where we'd ever lived. That's how the fight started. Somewhere in the middle of it, I asked, "Why are you always so angry?"

"I'm not angry!" he shouted.

"Are you still angry over Paul's death?" I asked.

"There were things that made me angry long before your brother died." There was a silence. I could see Dad looking at Mom in the rearview mirror as if to say help.

"Like what?" I started fishing. I thought if I could understand the anger that drove him to yell at us, beat us, and throw us around as kids, I could forgive him. I was sure I could. I asked if it was the war. Although he'd fought in the Battle of the Bulge, he seldom talked about it. He didn't answer. I asked if it was Grandpa, who used to beat him with a garden hose. He kept scratching his head, adjusting his glasses.

I must have worn him out with my questions, and I think I wore my mother out, too, because when I finally got around to asking, "Did Grandpa approve of Mom?" she blurted out, "He didn't want your father to get married again."

"What? *Again?*"

The car lurched left. I felt like someone had rammed a fist in my stomach.

"You were married *before?*"

No answer. My father steeled his concentration on the road as if he had no more peripheral vision. In the place where I used to reach over and pat his thigh there was a wall.

"What happened to your—" how could I say the word "wife" in front of my mother?

"She died."

"Harvey—tell her the truth."

No, don't tell me the truth, I thought, or everything you've ever told me will feel like a lie.

"We were divorced."

I felt the sudden intrusion of the pronoun "we." I wanted to know who else that "we" included, but at the same time I didn't. I asked anyway.

"Did you have any children?"

Silence.

"Did you?" Tell me. Please don't tell me.

"I had a daughter."

"Had a daughter?" Another fist. It felt like the scissors, paper, rock game I used to play with my brothers, only every sentence was rock.

"What happened to her?"

My father turned to look at me.

"The next thing you'll be asking is whether you're adopted." There was hatred in his eyes.

"What?" I looked back at my father. His hard eyes were back on the road, his peripheral vision gone again. I looked at his angular nose, then ran my finger along the angles of my own. Oh my God, I thought, am I the daughter from that other marriage?

"Mom?" I spoke to her through my sideview mirror. "Am I adopted?"

"Of course not," she said, but her voice didn't convince me.

My father started coughing, hard, and didn't really stop until we pulled up in front of my cousin Bob's house. The car slowed to a stop, and Dan pulled up in the car behind us.

I bolted from my parents' car and flew into Dan's arms. If I were going to a family reunion, I needed to walk in with the one person I knew for sure was family, if not by blood, at least by marriage.

I entered my cousin Bob's house feeling as if my uncles, aunts, and cousins were suddenly strangers. While talking with my cousin Nancy, I watched my father lean over to whisper something into her father's ear. Uncle Harry, my father's younger brother, has always been my favorite uncle. I wondered if he knew. My parents behaved in their distressingly ordinary way throughout the reunion. I was bursting with secrets, huge with doubts.

That night, I lay awake next to Dan, crying with a pillow over my face so my parents wouldn't hear me in the room next door. I cried for the sister I'd never met, for the father I'd never really known. I cried for my mother, wondering if she was really my mother, or if my mother was someone I'd lost long ago in some vanished part of my life. I cried hardest over that, because truthfully, if I had to trade in a parent, I don't think it would have been her.

The next day I made my father tell me for sure whose daughter I was.

"Mine," he said, stifling a cough.

"But you still haven't told me who my mother is," I protested.

"Don't be silly," my mother said.

Later, I learned that my father's oldest daughter, Joanne, was alive and living in Wisconsin. My father told me the story between fits of coughing. I was relieved that Joanne, not I, was the child of another mother. But I felt replaced, if not in my father's affections, at least in position. I was no longer his first girl. I now had a sister who was twelve when I was born. My father hadn't seen Joanne in thirty-some years, since she was six years old. Another man had adopted her.

"Why did you make it sound like I was the one who was adopted?" I asked.

"I didn't want you asking any more questions," he said.

What questions could have been so awful that it was worth making me doubt my own birthright? I needed to know if he loved this daughter, if she was the heartache that had made him so mean.

"What was she like?" I asked.

"She was a dancer," he said. "She had good legs, legs like yours."

I crossed my legs for some reason, put one hand over each knee. I didn't know who he meant—his first daughter who was six when he last saw her, or his first wife who must have been in her early twenties when they split. But with my mom standing there, self-conscious as she had always been about *her* legs, I didn't dare ask any more questions.

The flight attendant comes by and taps me on the shoulder, motions to me to lift my tray table and restore my seatback. I don't know how long I've been sitting here in a stupor, my book open in front of me. I look down at my notes. I've written one line of Beethoven's first song, *To an Infant* and that's it. If I have to give the first lecture on Beethoven tomorrow I'll have to wing it. I write down the rest of the words to the song: "You do not know who prepares the swaddling clothes, who it is that warms you and gives you milk. You grow in peace nevertheless. Within a few years, among all those who have cared for you, you will learn to distinguish your mother."

AUGUST 1992, DENVER

I see my doctor walking toward me down the hall. A small child, blond, is holding her hand. It is her two-year-old son, Alex. It's Sunday, and Dr. Grant is supposed to be off, which is why she doesn't have a sitter.

I have been extra-suicidal—plans, the whole bit. Part of me wants to do it, bad. Another part of me doesn't. I've had full privileges and passes for a week. It would have been so easy to walk through the three sets of locked doors and out the front entrance. Interstate 225 is about two blocks away, the overpass high. I've always wanted to sky-dive, descend through the clouds like a falling angel, but I never trusted the promise that my parachute would open. Better to jump off the bridge over the highway, wave to the setting sun dropping behind the mountains, a choice instead of a broken promise.

"But what if some poor construction worker driving under the bridge ends up with a dead body in the back of his pickup?" Sherry had asked.

I said she had a point, but I didn't expect her to rat. You get all your privs yanked just for talking about it around here.

Dr. Grant is leading me outside to the courtyard. Picnic table therapy, I guess. She wants Alex to run around and play while we talk. The high brick walls make it safe for him, safe for me. I watch this little kid stumble around in his pee-wee cowboy boots, his plastic guitar slung over his shoulder, and I want to say, "Enjoy it while it lasts, kid. You'll get yours someday." But then I see him look at us and smile, run up to his mother—my doctor—and give her a hug and I know I'm wrong. Not this kid. He'll be fine because he's protected. Until adolescence. Then he'll rebel against his psychiatrist mother by forming his own rock group, the Locked Doors.

"So what's making you want to hurt yourself?" Dr. Grant asks.

I don't answer. I'm tracking Alex. "Somebody should be watching him."

"He'll be fine," she says, "but you're not. What happened?"

I can't take my eyes off Alex. I want him to fall or something, to prove that his mother is just as neglectful as mine.

"You were about his age when your mother told you to go away, weren't you?"

"No," I answer defensively. "I was at least two and a half, maybe three."

My mother was huge. It was just before my sister was born. I can't believe she's bringing this up after I told her I couldn't talk about it anymore. I'd drawn a ghost in art therapy, or an angel disappearing, floating off the upper-left edge of the paper. Underneath the angel I'd written the words "Go away, just go." Dr. Grant asked me what the words meant. Those were the words my mother said when she found me in her bed with my father, I'd said. I told my mother it wasn't my fault, and please don't be mad, but she was worse than mad. She was crying *and* mad. She told me to get out. "Go away, just go," she'd said. Dr. Grant asked me where I went after my mother said those words. "Heaven," I told her. She asked me if I thought I'd died. I said I was already dead in my father's bed. Later, I remembered hearing the door slam and standing on the other side of it. "It really *was* my fault," I told her. I'd gone into my parents' bedroom to find my mother's perfume. I wanted to smell like her for church. I saw the square bottle on her dresser (Intimate by Revlon, I'd later learned), but my father came out of the shower and found me before I could reach the perfume.

"Is that what made you want to go away for good?" she asks now.

I don't answer. I watch Alex pet a fuzzy dandelion and sing to himself as the threads of spun silver float up through the air.

"You were remembering your mother's response to catching you in her bed with your father. Is that what made you want to hurt yourself?"

Couldn't I die and come back as Dr. Grant's kid? I would be so good, except when I wasn't, and then I would only be half-bad.

"She should have thrown him out, not you, you know."

"Right," I say. "Why don't you tell her that?"

"Your mother doesn't believe you," she says, "why should she believe me?"

For some reason, this makes me laugh, but it is a forced high-pitched laugh. It's the keep-away laugh. It's the "you can't come near me and you can't make me cry" laugh. It's the laugh I learned to force out when my father's belt ripped across my bare bottom, the laugh I'd learned from my brothers before their laughter turned into the howls of injured animals.

"That's funny?"

"I'm just thinking about what my mother believes," I say, still laughing.

"What's that?"

"Well, let's see. The last time I tried to kill myself, she wrote to me in the hospital to tell me I had demons."

"Do you believe that?"

"I did at one time. I believed we all had demons, my brothers, my sister, and I, and that's why we were all so depressed. I even had an exorcism during my freshman year of college—both my brother Paul and I had demons cast out."

"Did it work?"

"Obviously not."

"Have you ever considered that your mother might be nuts?"

"Briefly."

"Don't you think it's nuts to watch your husband beat and molest a child, then tell her she has demons and that's why she feels so bad?"

Alex is crying.

"Excuse me," Dr. Grant says. I watch her crouch down next to her son, who is holding the naked dandelion stem in his small fist. She hoists Alex into her lap, rocks him back and forth, and says soothing things into the top of his head. As I listen to the melodic rise and fall of her voice, I imagine her whispering about love and loss.

Watching this small child lose his first dandelion and get the comfort he needs from his mother, breaks the dam. By the time Dr. Grant returns to the picnic table my shoulders are shaking. The same hand that touched her little boy offers me a tissue. The other hand rests on my shoulder. I thought therapists weren't supposed to touch their patients, but just this once I'm glad she has broken the rule.

Once I have finally stopped crying, Dr. Grant points to the black journal sitting beside me on the table. I take it with me wherever I go, afraid I'll forget or disown whatever I don't write down. My journals are my defense against my mother's voice inside me which says, "This didn't happen. You just imagined it." I tell Dr. Grant that's what my journals are, my place to say "Yes, it did."

"Would you mind if I wrote something in it?"

Cheeky, even for a psychiatrist. No one writes in my journal except me. Still, I hand it to her. She opens it to the very back page, which is blank, and draws a line down the center of the page, then another across the middle. In the top left-hand box she writes, "Fantasy—nothing happened," and in the box underneath, "Bad Pain—price you pay." In the top right-hand box she writes, "Reality—yes it did," and in the box underneath, "Good Pain—feelings about any real thing that happened."

"We're going to be filling in these boxes," she says. "Suicidal feelings go on the left under 'It didn't happen.' Crying goes on the right under 'Yes, it did.'"

I look at the lines she's drawn like a cross in the back of my journal, at her writing, how it slants so far to the right, more printing than writing, and I just stare at the words she wrote in the upper-right corner, the three words I wished all my life my mother would say.

OCTOBER 1982, BOSTON

My brother David is still in the hospital. Instead of flying to New York last week, I should have flown to Florida. He had a list of people he wanted to come see him. Two weeks ago I was on it, but then, so was my brother Paul. Paul's been dead almost seven years. Now I'm not on the list. I wonder if Paul still is. I've been writing letters and calling daily, but my parents had just been visiting, and David barely talks to me now that they're gone. When he does talk to me he sounds so angry. Or he switches into that sarcastic, forced laugh. I recognize that laugh. "You gotta laugh so you don't cry," my sister Karen always said. And I remember my sister and me, sitting on the floor of the corner drugstore near the funny card section pulling cards off the rack to keep from crying. So when David makes jokes about the other patients—"No one gets lonely here because they all talk to themselves"—I know he is so lonely he could die.

What I do to get through this is what I have always done: practice. I'm working on the Liszt-Paganini Etude no. 6 and the Brahms Sonata in G for violin and piano, which I am supposed to perform with Sheila Fiekowsky, a violinist from the Boston Symphony. The Brahms is soothing, like falling rain. The Liszt is impossible, especially the right hand octaves in the fourth variation. As if that weren't enough, there's the sixth variation, with octaves in the left hand, double thirds and octaves in the right. Even the mighty among pianists have been undone by this variation. I rush like a madwoman, and then it's even more impossible. I don't know how I expect to conquer it. Maybe I don't, and that's why I'm working on it. Like a dog who's lost its master but wanders home, my fingers eventually find their way. The problem is, I get dizzy and have to stop playing at times. It's different from distraction, different from my mind going blank. More like a blackout.

David's wife, Vickie, says he was talking in group meetings at first. "He was talking about Baltimore," she said. Then my parents came. David stopped going to groups. When Dr. Kaye interviewed them and asked if there had ever been any trauma in our family, my father said no. Vickie protested. "Your oldest son hanged himself six and a half years ago," she said. Dr. Kaye raised his eyebrows at my father. "David didn't even go to the funeral," she continued, "and he thinks Paul is still alive."

I'm glad there was someone there to tell the truth. Apparently, my mother confessed that when David was in the second grade, the school psychiatrist said he needed help, but they didn't do anything about it. They didn't believe in therapy, she said.

They still don't believe in therapy. Vickie said one of the last things she heard my mother tell my brother David before she left the hospital in West Palm Beach was "This is a pretty expensive hotel you're staying in." She said when my father left the hospital for the last time, David begged him not to go, and stood in front of the door. My father pushed him out of the way, pulled the locked door shut, and left David standing on the other side.

Before my parents visited David in the hospital, I'd written him a letter to confirm that the things he'd remembered about Baltimore were facts, not hallucinations. I told him I remembered the beatings, too, how crazy and violent and out of control Dad was. I told him not to think for a minute that *he* was crazy for remembering those things.

My brother showed my parents the letter when they came to visit him. I don't know if he was ratting on me or looking for them to confirm what we'd both remembered. My father flew into a rage. He called me from the hospital and yelled into the phone.

"How dare you write those things about me?" He didn't wait for my answer. "Did that feminist bitch therapist put these ideas into your head?" I have learned to hold the phone away from my ear at times like this, but I wasn't quick enough. "All I can say is you'd better not try to have children of your own." Then he handed the phone over to my mother.

"You've hurt your father terribly," she said.

"Mom, please, I was trying to help—"

"Until you restore the warmth in your voice and stop saying such hurtful things about your father, I don't wish to talk to you."

"I was trying to help David," I said. "Isn't he the one who needs help?"

My mother didn't answer. Since then, no one in my family talks to me. My mother writes "how could you" letters on behalf of my father, who refuses to write or talk to me until I apologize. I am the family traitor, not just for being in therapy, but for daring to confirm that my brother David's memories were true.

I want to wake Paul up from the dead, so he can speak up for David's memory, and for mine. Maybe that's why David wanted him to visit. He'd always looked up to Paul. Paul was the golden boy, the standard-bearer my father always held up to us. The problem is that Paul's last act was hanging himself. What kind of standard is that?

We've all felt suicidal at one time or another in my family. My mother says we get it from her side of the family. My mother grew up with a mother who was constantly threatening suicide. While they lived in Texas and Arkansas, my grandmother had these "nervous spells." My mother and her sister and brothers could not fight or raise their voices in front of Grandma for fear of setting her off, for fear that she might try again to kill herself. I learned from one of my cousins that one of Grandma's worst spells took place while the family was living in Texas. Grandma's alcoholic father was living with them. Grandma found him drunk and in bed with a family member, a young girl, and told him to get out. After that she went crazy, threatening to kill herself.

My mother told me once that she envied Paul because he was in heaven and out of pain. I never understood that, not completely. I would think you'd just feel devastated if your own son committed suicide, not envious. My parents *must* have been devastated. My sister saw my father cry. I never saw him cry. I wish I had, because when I saw him dressed for my brother's funeral in his black velvet robe with the purple satin vestments, I felt sick. I wanted him to let someone else bury my brother. I wanted him to sit in the pew with his family and sob. Instead we listened to him deliver the eulogy for his own son. My mother just sat in the pew like stone. She wore a navy blue suit, not a black one, as if she wasn't going to fully give in to mourning. For a long time afterward she couldn't make decisions about the smallest things. She'd spin around in circles in her own kitchen trying to figure out what to cook for dinner, just kind of staring off into space. I wanted to stop her long enough to get her to look at me, long enough to put my arms around her and say, "It's okay, Mom, it's going to be okay." A person has to let that sort of thing in, but she never could, at least not with help from me. What I really wanted to say was "Please stay here, Mom, stay *here* with the living."

It's funny sometimes, the way you can trick yourself into staying alive. The last time I spoke to David I tried to reassure him by talking about my own hospitalization, which took place almost two years ago. I was trying to say, "Look, I got through this, so can you." But like the letter I'd sent, it backfired.

"You signed in," he said.

"What difference does that make?"

"Look, you chose to be in the nut house. I didn't."

"*So what*," I yelled into the phone. "I'm alive, you're alive. Isn't that the most important thing?"

His silence weighed more than anything he could possibly have said.

My brother is right, I did sign myself in, but I thought I'd done it to save my marriage. Dan had caught me counting pills in the bathroom. It wasn't the first time. Of course, if I'd taken all the pills, there wouldn't have been a marriage to save. My therapist said, "You got yourself hospitalized to find out what your brother Paul could have done to get help."

In January 1980, it had been four years and one month since Paul's death. I still saw him everywhere I went. I would burst into tears when I realized it wasn't him. I would wake up in the middle of the night confused, calling his name, surprised to find Dan in bed with me. It was my last semester of grad school at New England Conservatory, my marriage was straining at the seams, and I couldn't concentrate on my studies or my practicing.

All I know is, I tried to get help from the wrong person. Dr. Thomas had been recommended by a friend, actually the former assistant chaplain from my college. I knew my parents were against therapy, that they thought it was too secular, so the fact that this therapist was at a divinity school in Cambridge was a plus. I liked him immediately. He had my brother Paul's charm and intelligence, and more credentials than my father. He listened intently, and empathetically. Since he, too, was a minister's son, he said he understood all the theological underpinnings of what I was going through. He said there was a way to hold on to my belief in God through all this and come out stronger. I believed him. I fell in love with him, too, the way you might fall in love with any man who would listen to your story for hours and hours and still sound interested, the way you might fall in love with any man who is so eloquent, the way any woman might fall in love with a male therapist. I felt, too, that in Dr. Thomas's presence, the best of my brother Paul was back, and at the same time, I'd gained the kind of father I'd always wanted.

I'd been in therapy three months when I went with my mother-in-law to see the new East Wing of the National Gallery in Washington, D.C. I was wearing the dress she'd just bought me—a fitted white knit with red trim and a narrow skirt slit up the sides, something I would never have chosen for myself, but wore because Mil picked it out—that and red high-heeled sandals with tiny thin ankle straps. I was looking at a Rothko painting, staring at colors so vivid they seemed to pulsate, the way orange at sunset moves and shifts into purple and pink. It was an orange you could almost taste, sink your teeth into, blood orange. It filled me with wonder, and stirred something deep and primal inside me. I feared the danger of that kind of beauty, beauty that made me so quiet and unable to move.

I was standing in front of that painting when Dr. Thomas walked in. He tapped me on the shoulder, and I must have turned toward him with a look of love and wild fear on my face. I felt naked. He was the last person I expected to see, and yet it seemed as if I'd been waiting for him. He studied me as if I were the painting he'd come to see—a woman in red and white standing in front of purple and pink and orange, instead of a patient in brown flannel and blue jeans who'd come to see him week after week. In that moment, and maybe for the first time in my life, I knew I *was* a woman. I knew the power of it. I was both astonished and terrified. What I saw in his eyes told me that he had crossed some invisible line toward me and I would never be the same.

"Beautiful, aren't they?" he said, extending his arms to the walls surrounding us.

"Oh, yes," I answered. "I can't take my eyes off this one."

He stood beside me and we both looked into the vibrating orange, then he brushed my shoulder lightly with his hand and guided me around to the painting behind us.

"This is my favorite," he said, pointing.

I looked across his outstretched arm, followed it beyond the tip of his index finger.

I saw her then. My mother-in-law was walking toward us.

I felt caught, and yet proud to introduce Dr. Thomas to this woman he'd heard so much about.

"He's lovely," Mil said later as we walked out of the Rothko exhibit. I realized that he was poised in years halfway between us, a man she and I could both equally appreciate as a work of art.

"He's the therapist who has helped me so much," I said, knowing that everything would be different the next time I saw him, wondering if she had understood what had just taken place and in her gracious way left it alone.

Dr. Thomas's first letter came a few weeks after we'd met at the Rothko exhibit. He hadn't talked openly yet about his feelings for me during my therapy sessions, but it was there, in his eyes. The letter frightened me. I didn't want him to say in words what he'd said with his eyes, and with his embraces at the end of my sessions.

"Do I want to write what most respectable therapists are afraid to write—that successful therapy, religious awakening, and falling in love are all of a piece. . . . Why should the religious scholar flee from the sensuous poetry of the mystic who feels so vividly the passion of divine union and can find no better words than the image of sexual completion. And why should the psychotherapist flee from the powerful feeling of a loving and prized therapeutic encounter and have to name it so prosaically as transference that must be worked through? The therapist must find a way to say good-bye, to release the client into a world of relations with others, but should that mean never genuinely saying hello?"

If he had simply stated that he loved me, and that, since we were both married, it would be wrong, that would have been easier than all of those confusing questions about transference and divine union. I wasn't ready to say good-bye, but I wasn't sure I was ready to say hello in the way that he meant it, either. But I wonder if we'd already said hello at the Rothko exhibit. When I wore that white dress with the red border and high heels, I felt as if I were playing dress-up. It's the same way I feel in a concert gown. But when the music ends, I usually return to my jeans and flannel shirts.

Our sessions had changed after the Rothko exhibit. There were embraces at the end that lasted longer and longer. I'm not sure what I wore to those sessions, but it wasn't flannel. All I know is I must have tried to hold on to Dr. Thomas in whatever way I could. Did I play the part of the coquette instead of the truly depressed and grieving young woman I was? I don't know. I couldn't afford to lose someone my life depended on, and I felt my life was fully in his hands. He was the only man in whose presence I could utter the words, "My brother is dead," without going to pieces. And I wanted him to love me in the same way my brother had, but not leave.

I don't know what made Dr. Thomas fall in love with me. That part wasn't supposed to happen, and I've often wondered what I did to bring that on. He wondered, too. In one of the many letters he wrote me he asked, "What is it that enchants me so?" Then, like a laundry list—"Your warmth? Your smile? Your talent? Your openness? Your support? Your way of responding to life?" I wasn't sure which thing to feel guilty for. Maybe I felt guilty that he appreciated me at a time when Dan didn't. He said there had been a lot of "synchronicity" between us—"Jung's term for the graceful and almost mystical timing of things coming together at the exactly appropriate moments."

Which moment was it? "One day—so clear and so vivid throbs through my consciousness." He wrote that letter much later while listening to "Elisabetta's aria" from Verdi's *Don Carlo*, he told me. "A height of arching space—a pure white dress and bordered round with red, a delicate unfolding flower . . . there in the prints we hover as if enchanted in a world of private splendor—" That must have been the Rothko exhibit. If so, why do I feel so guilty? Neither of us knew the other would be there.

I don't know if that was the moment Dr. Thomas described in his letter, or if it was another. "An entry into ancient history—alone at first to see the gardens, and rooms of great antiquity—" he wrote, "so, too, a baron's ancient hall with instruments lain silent, yearning to know a master's touch to bring their strings to life."

That must have been later, at the Gardner Museum in Boston. I was getting ready for a concert there, Brahms *Liebeslieder* Waltzes, op. 52 for four singers and two pianists. Dr. Thomas had arranged to meet me at the museum a few days before the concert and when I ran up the stairs past the open courtyard to greet him, he picked me up off my feet and swirled me around, then kissed me. I started to sneeze. The courtyard was filled with white orchids. I am allergic to orchids.

The day of the concert I was fine, until the last song.

When the singers imparted the last phrase, "*Von Liebe, Lust und Leide, Gedenkt sie dein*" (my soul trembles with love, desire and grief when it thinks of you). My right hand trembled a little with the four eighth notes that accompanied each word.

Sharon Baker, the soprano, shot me a nervous sidelong glance, that look singers give when they feel the ground of the piano accompaniment giving way beneath them. Lucienne Davidson, the other pianist, played a little louder. When we bowed, I saw Dr. Thomas out in the audience, his daughter seated beside him near the back of the Tapestry Room, my husband seated several rows in front of them. I felt the tears well up. Once we exited the stage, Lucienne tried to comfort me, reassured me that it was our best performance. Dan brought me flowers. Dr. Thomas hugged me and introduced his daughter to Dan and me. She had beautiful raven black hair and was close to my age. It struck me that we could have been sisters.

Dr. Thomas also came to hear me rehearse for my master's recital at New England Conservatory. I was flattered by his interest in my music, the way he talked and wrote about my playing. "And music—that sweet power of the soul, that doth command the heart to open and the eyes to see. What precious gifts you have! You grace the lives of many, and in special ways, the sacred few, with the wonder of that opening." One of the pieces I performed was Schumann's Fantasy in C, op. 17. I told Dr. Thomas how the first movement was the most passionate thing Schumann had ever written. He was separated from Clara at the time, forbidden from even writing her letters, so he composed this music for her. Schumann penned a secret motto at the beginning of the piece: "Throughout all the tones of the earth there sounds one for him who hears in secret." At the end of the first movement, he wove in a melody from one of Beethoven's *Songs for the Distant Beloved* (An *die ferne Geliebte*) so that Clara would find the secret when she played it.

When I released my hands from the last chord, Dr. Thomas came over to the piano and sat beside me. He asked me who the distant beloved was for me. If there was a distant beloved for me then, it must have been my brother Paul. I felt shy and embarrassed about it, because he was my brother, not my lover, and he was dead. When I tried to tell Dr. Thomas that, he seemed upset. He told me he thought *he* was the distant beloved I'd been talking about. That's when he told me there would soon be real distance between us. He was moving down south.

Before my last session he wrote, "Doctor-patient tomorrow? Not quite. We are in a different place now and your well being is of far more than professional interest. We do stand on the same plane—and I know I would turn to you as readily as you turn to me, needing help—understanding, comfort, care . . ."

During my last session, Dr. Thomas did turn to me for comfort. He got up from his chair, walked toward me, then sat in my lap. I didn't know what to do, except to comfort him, which I did. I just held him in my arms and rocked him. With tears in his eyes, he told me he was in love with me. It felt so familiar and yet so wrong. He was married. I was married. I was a virgin when I married Dan. Dr. Thomas kissed me deeply and touched my breasts. My breasts had never been touched by anyone except my husband. When Dr. Thomas touched me, I felt a loss that was stronger than anything I'd felt since my brother Paul's death.

Before he moved, Dr. Thomas bequeathed several of his possessions to me: the rubber tree from his office, a tape of him singing Verdi's *Requiem* with the Tanglewood Festival Chorus, a carved linoleum block of a lion and a lamb lying side by side, not the print, but the block from which many prints had been taken, red ink still caked into the cracks, and a hollowed-out tree trunk that he had carved into the sensual curves of a woman's body. All of these things were what I'd loved best about him, the plant he'd nurtured and now wanted me to care for, objects he'd shaped with his hands that I could run my fingers over after he'd left, the sound of his voice blending with hundreds of others to make a music that would stay in my ears and my mind.

After Dr. Thomas moved away, he sent me love letters, poems, and Shakespearean sonnets. Every time I tried to get over him another letter would arrive. I would feel the intoxication at first, then the swift plunge into depression. "Yes, I know it's hard. It's hard for me. And what can stand as special? I've found some lines from Shakespeare I want to share with you:

> 'Now counting best to be with you alone
> then better that the world may see my pleasure
> Sometime all full with feasting on your sight
> and by and by clean starved for a look;
> Possessing and pursuing no delight,
> Save what is had or must from you be took . . .'"

I wrote him back more often than I wish I had. I was taking a course in English Romantic poetry at Harvard that summer. After two years at a music school I was hungry for words, and I wanted to be near Dr. Thomas in the only way I could. I walked by the divinity school as often as possible, trying to remember every embrace. In the middle of the summer, I was reading Coleridge's "Kubla Khan" and the image of a woman wailing for her demon lover haunted me. Eventually, I wrote Dr. Thomas to say that I had grown very depressed and suicidal, that my marriage was ruined, that I felt more alone than I'd felt in my life. I asked him to stop sending me love letters.

Dr. Thomas had a summer home in Martha's Vineyard, and I had promised to perform a benefit concert for the Martha's Vineyard Historical Society. I'd said yes at a time when I would have said yes to almost anything he'd asked. "I've prepared a place for you here," he wrote. Since he wasn't going to be there it seemed safe enough. Dan drove up with me, and we stayed in Dr. Thomas's summer home with his daughter, who was just starting college, the daughter we'd met at the Gardner Museum. The day after my performance the three of us went sailing in the family vessel. We sailed around Edgartown harbor in a rainstorm. When we returned to the house, Dr. Thomas's daughter took me to her bedroom to lend me some dry clothes. We were the same height, the same size. She opened a drawer and took out the clothes, and from another drawer, a folded up piece of white paper. She wanted to read me a poem her father had written for her. I changed into her clothes and sat on her bed with her, happy that she felt close enough to share something so intimate. As I listened, I slowly realized it was the identical poem he said he'd written for me. I could hardly bear to listen to the end. It felt as if he'd betrayed his daughter and me with the very same words.

After Dan and I returned home, I sent my copy of the poem back to Dr. Thomas, along with the most sexually explicit letters he had written me. I never asked for the letters

I'd written him, or the tapes of my playing I'd given him. I don't know if he kept them or not.

There was only one part of me that Dr. Thomas didn't have.

After the Rothko exhibit, he'd told me he wanted to start taping our sessions. He said my experiences and the way I articulated them were extraordinary. He wanted to preserve my voice, have it on tape.

I said no. It was the only thing I would not give him. I gave him tapes of my playing, I gave him access to my body and soul, but I would not give him my voice. If I had given him that, he would have had all of me. I kept the one part of myself that would enable me to go on without him. Some self-preserving angel inside me whispered, and when pressed, shouted, No. It is one of the few times I can remember saying that word with complete authority.

I kept my voice.

After I began teaching at Northeastern University that fall, the letters came more slowly. In November, Dr. Thomas wrote to tell me he'd decided to work things out with his wife, and asked me to return the linoleum block carving of the lion and the lamb.

The following January I checked into a general hospital west of Boston. I stayed in a room which reminded me of a college dorm, only the psych ward had just been painted, which made me wonder what had been written on the walls before. Graffiti? Last wills? Pictures? Whenever I smell fresh paint, I wonder what's underneath it. And now the smell always reminds me of that place.

Dan came to visit me daily, even brought a dozen roses for Valentine's Day, which made me cry. I made him a card from the art therapy room, a watercolored pink heart with blue streaks running through it.

My parents never visited me there. They called once to say "How could this be happening to our lovely talented daughter?" My mother asked me how I could do this after all they had done for me. My father called me his "Paderooski." And for some reason I asked him, "If I stopped playing the piano would you still love me?" He said he would, that I had many other talents under my fingers, like art, but that he hoped I'd continue playing the piano. When I'd tried to quit once in high school, he was adamant. But something in his tone of voice had changed. He seemed less sure of himself, more scared to push me about music.

After my parents' phone call, I became obsessed with my hands. I spent hours in the art therapy room, drawing my fingers through wet clay the same way I'd drawn them across the keys of my piano. I made several impressions, drawing out legato lines, making long channels in the clay, like a cat hanging on to a wall for dear life, slowly dropping, leaving a trail of claw marks behind in the plaster.

I stayed for ten days. Went to groups, went to therapy, worked with clay.

In my exit interview, my psychiatrist asked me if I was still feeling suicidal.

"Not at the moment," I answered, "but I'm sure it will always be a temptation."

He looked at me, made a few notes, then said, "Isn't it odd to call suicide a temptation?"

"I don't think so," I said. "Remember when Jesus was tempted in the wilderness? The devil asked him to throw himself off a cliff."

"Well," he said, looking at me over the tops of his glasses, "I don't know about that, but temptation isn't ideation, is it?"

I had no idea what he was talking about, but I shook my head that no, it wasn't, agreed to attempt therapy again, and he let me go.

When I got home from the hospital, I went straight to the piano. A slant of sunlight fell across the keyboard, and at first I just brushed my fingers across the ivory. I sat there for a long time, making shadows on the keys. I'd been away from the piano for ten days. I started back to work, sounding out the opening chords and arpeggios of Beethoven's *Emperor* Concerto, which I was scheduled to perform in a month. I couldn't think of much else to live for, so I decided that until I could find other reasons, I'd live for the next performance, then the next, and the next.

The things I learned from that brief stay in the hospital all had to do with hands: (1) Unless my hands were busy I felt worthless; (2) if I couldn't move my hands at a piano, I could move them through clay; and (3) I needed to find a therapist who would keep his hands off me.

When I did find a therapist, she promised that she would never fall out of her therapeutic chair into my lap. And I found a clay sculpting class. I loved throwing the huge clump of clay onto the table, and letting it take its own shape. I formed a sarcophagus out of the first lump of clay, and dug out six openings. I rolled a ball of clay into a tiny stone and laid it in one of the holes, the way you'd lay a sleeping baby down in a crib, then fired it in the kiln.

I still have that clay piece. I put it down in the basement because it was too hard to look at. My basement is like a mausoleum where I stash everything I want to hold on to, but don't want to see all the time. My brother Paul's cross-country skis are there. Old woodies that I should throw away, but don't. Once in a while I go down there to check on things, to rub the bottoms of his skis, or to pick up that clay piece, make sure the stone hasn't moved. Dr. Thomas's hollowed-out tree trunk is there, too. Sometimes when I run my finger along the carved out insides, the two vacant knotholes, the subtle curves opening up to the hollow inside, I think it is me. I was his tree to carve, and the sculpted shell is all that remains.

My hospital stay was a lot shorter than my brother's. They're letting David out in a couple of weeks, if they can determine he's no longer dangerous to himself or others. But how will they know? My parents took the gun, the one he'd threatened to kill his wife and son with, the one he might have turned on himself, and said they are going to sell it. But he can always buy another one.

My parents have been telling my brother that all he needs is a new job. It was that graveyard shift that did it, my father says, sleep deprivation. My mother says that we're all genetically depressed and there's nothing that can be done about it.

My sister is afraid she is next in the breakdown lane. Three down, one to go. I'd tell her not to worry, that I think she'll be okay, but she doesn't want to talk. Maybe she thinks she'll catch it from me, whatever *it* is.

I think of her while practicing the fast octaves in the fourth variation of the last Liszt-Paganini Etude. During her senior year of college, her right arm hurt her so badly while she practiced the piano that she had to quit playing. My right arm has been hurting for weeks. I hear Leonard Shure's voice from my last lesson. "You have to throw the octaves," he said. I imagine myself winding up at the pitcher's mound, throwing octaves to the batter, hoping one of them will make it into the strike zone.

And I think of the time my brother David tried to throw a stone at my father, who was behind the camera. I remember the photograph. It was taken in Baltimore. We were all standing out in the backyard dressed in our church clothes. And there was David, his seven-year-old face all scrunched up, his right arm cocked, his little fist closed around the rock.

I move the weight on the metronome back a few notches, try throwing the octaves slower. My right arm still hurts, and I'm starting to feel dizzy again. Dan sticks his head in the door. "Hurry up," he says, "we're going to be late."

Dan's voice brings me back to the present. I'm grateful.

We walk down the street to the Browns' house. We're going to press apples for cider with Eric and Meri. Eric and his brother Keith haul out the old wooden apple press they've had for years. Keith with his blond curly hair and blue eyes reminds me of Paul, and for a moment I pretend that he and Eric are my brothers. I imagine the Brown brothers as little boys, blond and brunette, lifting each other high to toss in the apples while their father turns the crank. They are caught up the way little boys are, and maybe in their enthusiasm they throw in too many at once. Their father reprimands them, but lovingly, with a pat on the head.

Meri and I throw in the apples, while Eric, Keith, and Dan take turns heaving the crank around. A lacy golden foam appears in the wooden tray below, and I follow Meri's example and dip my finger in to taste. The nectar is sweet, but salty. I swallow hard, more times than I need to, then realize I am swallowing tears I've been storing for weeks.

"It's strange how apples can make you cry," I say.

Meri puts her arm around me.

"I know," she says. "I know."

AUGUST 1992, DENVER

Today is my first journal group. Strange, to be joining a group to write. I can't imagine joining a group to practice the piano—the cacophony of sound would be terrifying. Practicing the piano and writing are lonely acts. They are meant to be done in private. And yet they are the very acts that keep me from feeling entirely alone.

Kathleen Adams, author of *Journal to the Self*, leads the group. When she gave me my screening interview, I told her I was already a writer, I'd been writing in journals for most of my life, and I'd just completed a novel, *In Sanctuary*, while in residence at the Writers' Room in Boston. I told her all of that instead of saying, "The last thing I need right now is your stupid journal-writing group."

I have, after all, lost most of my dignity in this place. Writing, for me, is an embodiment, a second skin. It covers the vulnerability and still exposes what needs to have light. Along with practicing the piano, writing is the thing that's kept me alive.

I told Kathleen I needed to keep my writing private, the same way I'd kept my practicing private. Instead of trying to persuade me to join, Kathleen asked me if I knew Dan Wakefield from the Writers' Room. Surprised, I said yes and asked how she knew him. "We've conducted journal writing workshops together." She was appealing to the snob in me rather than the mental patient. It worked. I signed up for her group.

Today, she asks us to write about a recent dream, then pair off and tell the dream to our partners. Our partners will then ask us questions that we will not answer directly, but write down instead. We will answer the questions in a poem.

I get stuck next to Alice, who is typing in Braille. Her head is raised as if she is looking for her dream through closed eyelids. The typewriter is so loud I can't think. It reminds me of my mother's typing, late at night, a long time ago.

Every Saturday night my mother typed my father's sermons. I remember lying in my bed hearing the metal letters strike the platen and the bell preceding each carriage return. I wondered how many bells before my father would enter my room. I'd lie awake pretending to sleep, praying the bells would stop ringing soon.

I try to shut out the sound. I wish I were holed up in my quiet room, writing in solitude.

Eventually, I get the dream down. I was moving, again. I have moved so many times in my life that the dreams are commonplace. But still, I am filled with the old terror that everyone and everything I love will disappear. The night before the moving van was to come, I stood on the porch and saw my landlord in the driveway in a convertible sports car with the top down. He was groaning, yet trying to keep his voice low. I saw the body of a woman, then her head down between his legs. When the landlord let out his final groan, and the woman came up for air, I saw the face of one of my cousins. I stood there for a moment staring, then screamed at my cousin to get out of the car. Then I watched my dog, Nicky, run across the lawn toward me. I apologized to the landlord that my dog had run across his lawn, then felt sick that I had apologized. I told the landlord to get out, too. The landlord leaned back in the driver's seat, then didn't move. He had become my father.

I tell Alice my dream, wishing that she could see my face as I speak. She sits quietly, hands resting on her Braille typewriter, then looking up as if she could half-see me asks: "Is the landlord really your father? Who is your cousin? Why did you apologize to the landlord about the dog? Who is the dog?" I write down her questions, then wait for more.

"I guess I'm not very curious beyond that," she says, then tells me her dream.

When the dream-telling and questions are over, I sit for a long time staring at Alice's questions, wondering how I am supposed to compose a poem from a list of who's who. I feel the old longing to write a beautiful poem, knowing that I have never been, and will never be, a poet.

"The point is not to write the perfect poem," Kathleen says out loud, looking right at me, but directing her comments to the whole group. "The point is to learn from your dreams."

I begin to write. I cross out every line until I end up with something that, while not a poem, at least contains some truth.

Although I have read my writing in public before, when it is my turn to read my writing out loud, my mouth is dry as cotton.

> *You are the landlord*
> *and I am the fool*
> *for believing that anyone or anything*
> *ever belonged to me.*
> *The lowest of God's creatures loves me best.*
> *And you, God's servant,*
> *dressed in black,*
> *ringed round the neck with white,*
> *have stolen my soul.*
> *Still, like a dog,*
> *I always come back.*

After I finish, Kathleen asks me to give it a title.

"Betrayal," I whisper.

And then I imagine him, the childless priest behind the screen, the screen we Protestants were never allowed.

"Father, I have sinned," I would say.

"What is this sin, daughter?" he would ask with kindness. And since I would be Catholic, not Protestant, and the priest could not be my real father, I would no longer be afraid.

"I told, Father. I told."

"Breaking Silence" is my hardest group. I haven't been able to stay all the way through. Maybe today.

Judy asks for a volunteer to read the statement of purpose. I'm feeling brave today, so I raise my hand.

I clear my throat, take a deep breath. I know every woman here is looking down.

"To talk about incest," I say, "the violation of a child's innocence by a parent or sibling through any unwanted touch, vaginal, anal, oral—" I stop, feeling a catch in my throat. I think about the size of my mouth, how it was barely big enough to suck three fingers.

"I can't do this." I hand the paper back to Judy, our group leader. She hands it to Sarah who continues where I left off.

I am not here anymore. I hear the murmur of Sarah's voice. It is a running brook, and that's where I am. I'm sitting on the bank of the river, dangling my feet over the edge, wiggling my toes in the cold, cold water.

"Linda," I hear Judy's voice. "Linda, are you with us?"

Please, don't call me back. It's just fine here beside the river. The water is fine.

"I think it's important that you join us again—"

You know I can't talk. The last time you tried to make me talk, my teeth started chattering. Leave me alone.

"Why don't you open your eyes or give me a hand signal if you can hear me."

I raise my little finger, keep my eyes closed.

"Good. You don't have to talk. I'd just like you to stay here with us." I feel her rise and move toward the blackboard.

I hear the magic marker squeak. "Today we are going to talk about the cost of keeping silent—"

I hear my father's voice. We are inside the station wagon. I am sitting beside him.

"You know why I love your mother so much?" he says, and I want to know, but I don't want him to tell me. My mother is asleep in the back with my brothers and sister. It's so quiet you can hear the rhythmic breathing of sleep and the low hum of the engine. I'm not sure if it's B-flat or B-natural, and this thought occupies me while I wait.

"I love your mother because she knows how to keep silence in a thousand different languages."

I think of the verse in the Bible, the one where Saint Paul said "Let the women keep silence." I wonder if this is what he means or if it is something else. And I wonder what the different languages of silence are, and whether this is what God wants for women or whether it's just been misused. The hum of the engine lulls me. I pretend to fall asleep.

When I open my eyes, there is still this group. I look at my watch. I look up at the board. "Cost of keeping silent: suicidal feelings, self-mutilation, eating disorders"—the list goes on. I look around the room and know that for every woman here the cost is the same. We have all made attempts to take our lives, or to tell without words, some with a knife or a razor dividing the flesh, making the invisible somehow visible, others with the slow disappearance of flesh by starvation or underneath mounds of flesh—making themselves, and all they've been through, disappear. We have all kept our promises to remain silent, and marched slowly toward our own deaths.

I look up at the board. The word *death* is not up there.

"Is something troubling you, Linda?" Judy asks.

Just say it. Say the word. Say it here.

"My brothers kept their promises," I say, then look around the room until I find Judy's eyes, then Sarah's, then Sherry's.

"I wonder if that's why they're dead—they never told."

This is the first time I have spoken in this group. I'm surprised at the words coming out of my mouth. I'm surprised that I want to keep on talking.

"I suppose their deaths were more telling than anything they could have said, but that's just it. They're dead."

There. I've said the word twice, and I'm still here.

"What did the members of your father's church think when your brother David shot himself?" Sarah, one of the few who knows this information, does not spare me. A few new group members are wide-eyed.

"My father told them it was a car accident—"

"So even in his death he didn't really get to tell."

"What do you mean?"

"If your father lied about the way your brother died, then his death is another family secret." Sarah leans back in her chair. She is a veteran of hospitals, an old pro. More like a staff member than a patient, and sometimes more insightful than the group leaders. She is bored in groups unless she has a project. I am her project. I am oddly grateful.

"His story dies, too," she says. "Unless you tell it."

"The important people know," I say to the floor, mentally listing who they are: my sisters, my closest friends.

"Don't you think you have a moral obligation to tell the church?"

Now I look at Sarah directly. She has big, brown, demanding eyes. The kind of eyes you couldn't lie to and get away with it.

I don't answer.

"You know he molested you. What about your brothers? Were there others?"

"I don't know."

"Think of the Porter case. Think of the sheer numbers of children he molested in the church. Your father has incredible power beyond his own family—he has the trust of a whole congregation of families. What if you were not the only ones?"

"I can't answer that. I'm having enough trouble dealing with what he did to me without having to think about—"

My bottom lip is quivering. At any moment my teeth will start clicking together.

"Linda?" I hear Judy's voice, but it has gone far, far away.

The Morgans. Baltimore. I told the Morgans. I didn't mean to, it's just that I needed to know what had happened to Mr. Perch, the janitor in the Baltimore church. I called the

Morgans just before coming to Denver. It had been years since I'd talked to them. When I asked her about the church janitor, Mrs. Morgan told me he had been fired for molesting Sunday School children. I said it couldn't be true. He was so kind to children. I asked her who had made the accusation.

"Your mother," she answered.

I am five. I am running down the church stairs from my father's study. My hands are sticky. I have just wet my pants.

I am crying. I see my brother David at the bottom.

"Baby, baby, baby," he mocks.

I crumple into a ball at the foot of the stairs and cry harder. Mr. Perch, the church janitor, walks by. His skin is soft black and he has deep brown eyes, kind eyes. He crouches in front of me and wipes my eyes with a handkerchief. He takes my hands in his, then walks me to the bathroom. He is scrubbing my hands, hard, shaking his head, and saying "There, there," over and over. When he is finished, he holds both my hands, looks right into my eyes and says, "Daddies shouldn't do this to their little girls." I look at my hands inside his, and wish mine were black.

Right now another hand is touching mine, pulling me gently back to the group. I want to stay with Mr. Perch so he can show me the disappearing penny trick.

I hear Judy's voice. "I'm going to count slowly from five to one," she says. "By the time I get to one, you will be back in your safe place. Five . . . you are moving toward your safe place." I hear birds outside the window at Eric and Meri's house. "Four, you can see your safe place." The sunlight is strong. "Three, you are close enough to hear the sound of your safe place." I hear the voices of Benji and Jen, crying "Lindi, Lindi, read us a story—"

"Two, you can feel your safe place." This is the place where all children are safe, where I am safe. There is comfort here. It is the in-between place, the place between past and present. "One, you can stay in your safe place now until you're ready." Now that I'm here I know it is safe to come back to the present.

When I open my eyes, Judy is looking at me, her brow all crinkled with concern. Sarah is gone. So are the others. Breaking silence is over, and this time I have stayed past the end.

"Tough group today," Judy says.

I nod.

"These are just ideas to think about," she says. "You don't have to act on any of them."

"I don't think I can."

"You don't have to," she says.

I look up at the board, which the next group leader is already erasing. I remember every word that was on the list, even the word that wasn't there. But that's not what scares me now. I'm not afraid for my brothers anymore. It's too late. I'm not afraid for my sister, who's a grown woman happily married. I'm not even afraid for myself.

I'm afraid for the ones for whom the church janitor lost his job. The new question, the one that makes my teeth rattle and my chest hurt, is whether my father might be a danger to anyone else. No longer does the secrecy affect only my life, whether I could stay in it or not with unbearable truths inside, but whether another life could be destroyed by my silence.

I remember reading an article about Father Porter's victims, how their overall lives had been affected. For some, there was the numbing with alcohol and drugs, for others, the inability to fully engage in their lives due to depression, insomnia, nightmares, and flashbacks, and for still others, the large number of suicide attempts. But what struck me most was something I'd never heard articulated by incest survivors, but was a common thread among Father Porter's victims: the existential aloneness of having been violated in the church by a man who was the representative of God. It is an aloneness that doesn't just put you outside of your own family, but outside the family of God.

I knew that aloneness. My brothers knew it. We'd each struggled to believe in the God our father preached about on Sunday. For every Saturday our father beat us, we were given the chance to ask his and God's forgiveness the very next day. For God, the Father, and our father seemed to be one. At the very least, our father, from up high in his pulpit, in his black velvet robes with the purple satin vestments, projected the image of God to us.

We hungrily accepted Christ into our hearts and our mouths. Communion was a problem because when my father said, "This is my body which is given for you," and put the bread in his mouth and commanded us to "Eat ye all of it," I felt so sick and confused, not remembering all those times he'd forced his body into my mouth, only remembering the yeasty taste of semen, the choking, the sucking for air. There in my pew, I would pray that God would come in only to find myself unable to swallow.

By the time I was in high school, I'd begun fasting. Crash dieting was a fad anyway, so I could hide my repentance and just look like one of the girls. But I was already thin, and when I fasted for even a day, I would pass out by the end of it. Before that happened, I'd get down on my knees or lie on my bedroom floor and pray that God would purify me—take away the shame and guilt I felt, not knowing why I felt it or exactly what I'd done.

Here were the sins I knew about: I'd smoked a little dope, I'd dropped some speed, I'd kissed a few boys deeply and touched places I shouldn't have, and I'd taken risks, done things that could have ended in death.

But banging my head on the concrete patio to knock myself out, slitting my wrist with a kitchen knife, taking every pill I could find in the house—these things seemed almost sanctioned by God. God, to me, was intrinsically bound up with my father, and I knew that my father would rather see me dead than hear me tell.

My brothers must have felt it, too. From the time I was twelve or thirteen, Paul had been talking about suicide, making attempts with his car or motorcycle, with drugs or booze, and all the while desperately trying to believe in a God he once called "the cosmic sadist." For my brothers, my sister, and myself, God was experienced through the crucible of family. In our family as well as the church, our father and "Our Father" were one.

If my father and God are one, then I am outside of every-thing—family, church, God's universe—there is nowhere to turn. My mother often said to me, "Your father and I are one." It felt like an impenetrable wall. I must need God the way I've always needed a mother—to love and comfort me, to nurture what is good, and to hate what is evil.

But good and evil are as bound together for me as reli-gion and sex. I remember, ten years ago, sitting in my living room with my best friend, Meri, and telling her there were two parts of my past I could never discuss with anyone: reli-gion and sex. I was crying when I said that. It's taken me ten years to understand why.

But in this moment, in this room, something is chang-ing. The cloth begins to tear. The cloak that has covered evil with good, sex with religion, begins to come off. And I won-der if there might be a God who is really the good Father, the Father who loves me. I need to believe that, and as much as I have needed a mother all my life, I also need a father.

I look at Judy's kind eyes, knowing I may never have this much support and safety around me again in my life.

"If I decide to report my father to the church, will you help me?"

Her face changes from concern to fear. I can see it in the furrow between her brows, the way it has just deepened beneath her shiny red bangs. She looks at me for what feels like a very long time.

"If that's what you decide to do," she says, "I'll be right there beside you."

The day I reported my father to the National Association of Congregational Churches was the day of my first canceled concert as a professional pianist. I can't say I planned it that way. Maybe it was an unconscious exchange—words for music. A breaking of the ancient bargain I'd made with my father. Instead of playing the piano, I told.

The concert I canceled was part of the Stockbridge Summer Music Series, where I've performed every summer for the past six years. The concerts take place in an old estate near Tanglewood. The piano is situated in a grand wood-paneled parlor in front of a huge fireplace, the kind you can walk into. Because of its close proximity to Tanglewood, many of the concerts have been chamber music with members of the Boston Symphony Orchestra.

In the summer of 1989, however, I performed a solo concert there. It was the beginning of my musical memory slipping, and memories from the past intruding. I began playing Beethoven's Sonata in E, op. 109, when my memory of the music slipped and I heard the footsteps I thought were my father's. After that, the memories became so constant and intrusive that I stopped performing solo concerts altogether. I couldn't risk the loss of musical memory, or the terror of past memories intruding during a performance.

The following summer, 1990, I performed Beethoven's *Archduke* Trio with Lucia Lin playing violin and David Finch playing cello. My mother, whom I had just told about the incest, was present for the concert. During the slow movement of the Beethoven, the quietest section of the Andante cantabile before the transition to the final rondo, a telephone rang. The phones in the estate house were usually switched off for the concerts. I remember thinking my father had somehow found us and was calling. In fact, he had just called a few days before to ask my mother what I'd told her.

"It was Baltimore," he'd said, "Linda's remembering Baltimore isn't she?" I assured myself that the fear of my father calling during a concert was irrational, and continued playing. The phone rang again, this time between the last two chords of the Andante cantabile. I startled, but with the music in front of me, began the Allegro moderato and kept playing to the end of the trio. After the concert, my mother said, "This is what I will remember from our visit—the music. The part you told me about your father I don't wish to remember."

I'd almost forgotten about this year's Stockbridge concert, the one I'd canceled, until Luci called to say she'd just finished playing. We were booked to perform the Brahms's Trio in B along with Fauré's Sonata for Violin and Piano and a jazz piece based on May Sarton's poem "The Phoenix Again" that

Claire Ritter had composed for Luci and me. Luci is my closest friend in music, a violinist who won a prize in the Tchaikovsky competition for playing like Heifetz, but isn't afraid to sling a Stradivarius low on her hips and play like Jimi Hendrix, either—something Claire had asked her to do when she was teaching us to improvise. Luci and I have played concerts together for seven years, since she first joined the Boston Symphony. But the friendship goes deeper than that. We've run and cycled together, walked our dogs together, played endless games of Scrabble, and helped each other survive everything from broken strings to broken engagements. The night before I left for Denver, Luci drove all the way to Boston from Tanglewood to help me pack for the hospital. We played Scrabble until dusk, then she drove me to the airport. At the gate, Luci literally had to shove me down the jetway and onto the plane. Now I am grateful.

On the phone, Luci graciously skipped over the details of the concert and described, instead, a recent bike ride she took through the Berkshires.

"How did the concert go?" I asked, not completely sure I wanted to know. I felt keenly the fact that I was in a hospital, not a concert hall, and given that I'd just broken the promise to my father, I wondered if I'd ever play the piano in public again.

"The Brahms went okay, " Luci answered. "It wasn't the same without you. Everyone asked where you were."

"Did you tell them I was in the nut house?" Some sense of humor was returning.

"No, but how's it going there?"

"I reported my father to the church today."

"You what?"

"Well, I didn't exactly tell the church. I called the Milwaukee office and spoke to a secretary. She told me she would speak to the Director of Pastoral Relations and get back to me."

"That was brave."

"I had help."

"It was still brave."

The secretary's name was Linda. I found that oddly comforting. I told her my story. She listened. She took me seriously. If no one else does, there will always be the memory of the voice at the other end, my namesake, who listened.

I can't believe I did it. I recite all the reasons: I did it to break the bond of secrecy between my father, my mother, and me. I did it for my brothers, in their memory. I did it to stay alive.

Maybe now I will be able to play the piano again, but for different reasons. Last night when I played in the cafeteria, I had a hard time finding my way around the keyboard. The piano feels so foreign to me now. It's strange. I remember only bits and pieces of things—Schumann's *Scenes from Childhood*, but not all of them, and sometimes not any of them. I have clear memories of things I'd forgotten for much of my life. Why can't I remember how to play the piano? My last public concert was just one year ago in Stockbridge. I'd performed the Dvorak *Dumky* Trio, again with Luci. Last night, I couldn't even remember the first chord—A minor? E minor?

I was hoping that calling the church might be an end—a transformation, the final healing. But it looks like it's just the beginning. Linda, the secretary in the Milwaukee office, says I will have to tell my story to someone who has the power to do something about it. I don't know if I'll have the strength to call again.

Outside in the courtyard, lying in the grass under a huge blue sky, I watch the clouds pass, make faces out of them. I imagine the face of God. As a child, I'd memorized hundreds of Bible verses. Now they run through my mind like music.

"Honor thy father and thy mother, that your days may be long on the earth," I remember, and suddenly doubt is back, thick and black, like the cloud that roamed through the houses of Israel, killing the firstborn of every household. What does it mean to honor your parents? To pretend that these things never happened or to love and forgive them in spite of knowing? Forgiveness starts with confessing your sins. But they have never asked my forgiveness. I was always ordered to ask my father's forgiveness, and for most of my life, I did. I was also ordered to keep silence. For most of my life, I did that, too.

But now I have told. My parents will say I am lying. They have never gone so far as to say that it never happened. "Our daughter wouldn't lie," my mother has said. "I'm sure something happened, but it wasn't my husband."

Last night Sandi came to visit me. I remember when she and my brother Paul were first married, how my parents used to drive all of us from Cheyenne to Denver for family dinners. With Sandi in the car, it was safer somehow. We behaved like a normal, almost happy family then. I was amazed by my parents' ability to make other people's children feel at home.

Sandi moved to Denver after Paul killed himself, and has lived here ever since, now with her two sons from her second marriage. For a long time after Paul died, Sandi still called my parents Mom and Dad. But now their relationship is strained. My parents know that Sandi and I are close, that Sandi knows my story, and through it, Paul's story, too.

"Your mom called me last night," Sandi said.

My stomach tightened. I waited. Apparently, my mother told Sandi that when we lived in Baltimore, she and my father had left the four of us kids with a baby-sitter for a week. "That's who molested Linda," my mother said. "We just thought you should know."

"Marge, I'm challenging you to at least entertain the possibility that what Linda is saying might be true," Sandi said.

"I can't do that," my mother replied. "It's just too much for me."

"It's sick, Lin," Sandi said to me. "Your best bet is to try and get healing for yourself—not to hope for any resolution with your parents." Sandi was a psychiatric nurse, and at one time had worked in the hospital where I'm staying. Although she was speaking in her clinical voice, there was sadness in her eyes, as if she were the one letting go.

I told Sandi my father had written me last summer to say it was the church janitor who'd molested me. The Baltimore church comes back, and with it memories of Mr. Perch.

Still lying in the grass, watching the clouds change shape and drift by, the Bible verses continue to play in my mind, like forgotten melodies that you suddenly begin to hum.

"Suffer the little children to come unto me and forbid them not, for of such is the kingdom of God." I pray to the sky that the healing Sandi described will come. A warm welcoming breeze envelops me, and I imagine the mural that was painted on the wall of a Sunday school room in the Baltimore church—Jesus pulling the children toward him, welcoming them into his lap. I never saw myself there, only other people's children, but now I see myself being gathered into his loving arms. I see my brothers there, too. I look for their faces in the clouds.

If I am healing, it is painfully slow. Unlike Saul on the road to Tarsus, there is no flash of light, and I am filled with doubt. After losing fifteen pounds in two weeks, maybe it's a good sign that I can finally eat in small bites, and don't take any more food off the plate than I can keep down.

But the day before I am scheduled to make the second phone call, I throw up twice, both lunch and dinner. I barely make it to the bathroom in time. My stomach hurts. It hurts full; it hurts empty. God help me, I pray. But there is only silence and the emptiness in my stomach.

Every week we meet in the same room for movement group, but this time I feel paralyzed. A folding partition slices the room in half and I feel closed in, claustrophobic. I tell Beth, the group leader, that I can't stay unless the partition is opened. I am learning to ask for what I need, which goes against everything I was raised to do.

My mother told me that once I learned to walk and talk I didn't need her anymore. "You didn't need anyone," she said, "you were so independent." I have always wanted that to be true. For years I believed it was true. It wasn't until two years ago, on the anniversary of my brother David's death, when the memories were intruding into every waking and sleeping hour that I asked for her help. It was the first time I can remember saying "I need you" to my mother.

She flew to Boston for two weeks, baked my favorite pies and cookies, helped organize my bills, attended three sessions with my therapist, Judy, during which I told her about the incest. There were moments of long-forgotten tenderness, like my mother letting me lay my head in her lap, the way she used to when I was small and she was removing the wax from my ears. I practiced Beethoven in the living room while my mother did dishes in the kitchen. This is the way my mother most often heard my music while I was growing up—over the clatter of dishes in the sink. I often hear whole measures of rests filled with the clanging of silverware underwater and my mother fishing for a fork or spoon to wash. She came to hear me play the concert in Stockbridge. When I told her my father had molested me at home and at church, regular as his Sunday sermon, she assured me she didn't know about it. She also told me, "If it were my father I'd never forgive him," then, "You've got to forgive your father," and finally, "My husband would never do that." Daughter, mother, wife, the three parts of her spinning like a gyroscope. In the last therapy session she told Judy, "My daughter doesn't lie, but if I believe her, I'll have to leave my husband, and I can't live without him."

The thing I needed most from my mother—to have her believe me—she couldn't give. Still, I was grateful for the two weeks we had without my father. And glad that I'd finally learned to say the word *need* without taking it back.

"I need you to open the partition," I say again to Beth.

"First we'll do check-ins, then we'll open it."

I sit on the floor waiting for the check-ins to end. I lean back against the folding partition and suddenly I am in the Sunday school room in the Baltimore church. The folding partition is closed, but I know the part of the room that's behind it, that leads to the bathroom where Mr. Perch washed my hands. I want to get up and find Mr. Perch, but I can't move.

Someone taps me on the arm. I jump up, and race out of the room. But there is no Mr. Perch. I am in a hospital, not a church. I end up at the nurse's station, out of breath. I ask for Ativan. Sharon, the nurse, says no. Instead, she asks if I'd like to talk. I am small and voiceless again, but without the chattering teeth. Progress. I shake my head, no, and walk back to my room. Sharon follows. When I am sitting on my bed she begins to count. But I don't want to go to my safe place. Before she gets from five to one, I blurt out the question that has kept me locked up since I told on my father.

"Will Mommy die?" My voice is small and vulnerable, like a little girl's. I'm ashamed that I've said "Mommy" not "Mother."

"What makes you think that?" she asks, not flinching at my choice of words or tone of voice.

I can't speak again. Whether it's fear of hearing the strangeness of my own voice, or fear of the answer, I'm not sure, but my voice has gone back inside. Sharon begins to count again, and this time she gets all the way back to one. I fall asleep.

When I wake up, I realize that today is my brother David's birthday. He would have been thirty-nine. He was twenty-nine when he died. If he had just waited one more month before he killed himself, he would have made it to thirty. He was afraid of his thirties. He was afraid of the two or three gray hairs he'd found that year. Sometimes I think if he'd just made it to thirty he would have lived. On the other hand, if his thirties had turned out like mine, he would have had reason to be afraid.

David was quiet a lot the year before he died, especially after he left the hospital. He'd been quiet at times all of his life. When we were little, the silences used to scare me. I would make faces to get him to laugh, or egg him on until he was angry enough to yell. Anything to hear his voice again.

In the last two years I have had these silences I haven't been able to break. It's not that I can't talk. It's just that I am afraid to talk. I think sentences to other people, I even hear my own voice in my mind, but I can't make myself talk. Ever since that time two years ago when I screamed out in the car, "Mommy, it wasn't my fault," with a voice that sounded five instead of thirty-five, there are periods when I'm afraid to talk. It's strange that it happened six months after I'd stopped seeing a therapist. Maybe if I'd shouted that out during a session she could have helped me. On the other hand, even when I was still seeing that therapist, and I tried telling her about my father's French kisses, which were as recent as the last time I saw him, she asked me, "Was that memory or fantasy?" I stopped talking about anything important after that, and asked for a new therapist. She sent me to Judy.

My friends get scared by my silence. For my birthday a friend of mine gave me a fountain pen and a small flip pad to use when I couldn't talk. Sometimes it worked, but sometimes it didn't. I write too fast and the thoughts are slow and stilted. I've tricked myself by using my left hand to write: Since the writing is more labored and takes longer, it's easier to get the thoughts down. But it looks like a child's scrawl, and I'm ashamed to have anyone see it.

I've thought a lot about the reasons my voice may come out small and childlike, the sentences simple and monosyllabic. Speech develops at an early age. If your speech has been silenced from an early age about events over which you had no control, then maybe when the ability to speak about these events returns, it is a child's voice because they are a child's questions.

The thing is, I don't feel I am someone else when my voice comes out like a child's. I am present the whole time. I am myself the whole time, but aware that I sound different, and it is embarrassing. It's a little like thinking a certain passage of music during a performance and having your fingers play something else. It's the closest thing to a memory slip that I've ever experienced outside of music. Memory slips in music were the reason I stopped playing from memory in public. Memory slips in my day-to-day life are the reason I've stopped talking.

Here, at the hospital, they encourage patients to talk in whatever voice they have. Some of the patients are not aware of who they are all the time, or who is talking. Sherry's voice is constantly changing, and huge spaces of time go by when she doesn't remember at all what she's said. I am grateful that this doesn't happen to me, that I am always present enough to hear the change in my voice and to keep my mouth shut.

It is a different kind of pain to be present in your mind but out of control in your body—to feel all the muscles in your back and neck tense the minute your head hits the pillow and the lights go out; to feel your lover's fingers near your throat and suddenly stop breathing; to feel his hand at the back of your head pulling you toward him and begin to tremble from head to toe, until he finally talks you back to the present; to see candles flickering on your birthday cake and hear your own teeth chattering until someone blows the candles out and tells you that, no, you are not in the church, your father is not holding a candle to your face, and you are safe.

This afternoon in my therapy session with Dr. Grant, we are talking again about safety. She is concerned about the incident in movement therapy, and the fact that I haven't been keeping down food.

"What good is it going to do you to report your father to the church if you jeopardize your own safety in the process?"

I tell her I'm not sure I can do it, but I'll probably be less safe if I don't.

"Why?"

"Because this is the only time I'm going to have this much support around me. I've already told the secretary. She's already passed it on. If I wait until I get home to tell, and my voice shrinks, or my teeth chatter, or I find a way to swallow enough pills, what am I going to do then? I'll be alone. This is my only chance."

"Well, I'm not sure what you're expecting, but be prepared for the possibility that you won't be believed, you won't be taken seriously, and that there may be repercussions we can't foresee."

"Like what?"

"Well, there's the possibility that your parents will never speak to you again."

"I'm not sure I ever want to speak to my father again."

"And your mother?"

I start to weep.

One month ago I wrote to my parents. Until then, I had not written or called in over a year, since my last suicide attempt and hospitalization in January 1991. My mother had sent me letters while I was in the hospital then, informing me that I had demons. The hospital psychiatrist strongly urged me to stop corresponding with my parents altogether until I was in a more stable place.

Last month, I thought I was. I wrote my parents a letter asking for a few cherished items that I thought I might never see again: a blue-and-white flowered teacup my mother reserved for me whenever I visited, a cassette tape of the chamber music concert I performed in Stockbridge the week after I told my mother about the incest, a photograph of myself with John Williams at my debut with the Boston Pops and, most important, a silver hand mirror that belonged to my grandmother. She lived with us every summer until she died, when I was thirteen. I felt safe and protected when she was around. My father behaved when his mother was in the house. But best of all, she loved me. She let me play with the silver mirror that always sat on her dresser. I'd look into it and for a few precious moments I was someone else.

I don't know if the items I asked my parents to send will be waiting for me at home. I suppose it was a little like asking for the things someone might give you after they die, before they're actually dead. After I sent that letter to my parents, I felt a sudden excruciating loss, as if I'd killed them by asking.

Last month, one week after I sent the letter, and one week before the anniversary of my brother David's suicide, something inside me just snapped. I took every pill I had: Prozac, Ativan, Fiorinal, Naproscyn—enough to do the job. I felt like a robot taking orders, no emotion about it. There was the writing out of some kind of will, to make certain my parents didn't get the house or the piano after I died, and the gradual loss of control over the pen.

A friend who'd been unable to reach me called Eric and Meri's to see if I was there. Eric showed up at my place, found me lying on the floor, and called the ambulance. Eventually, I ended up at Newton-Wellesley Hospital. I was getting to be a familiar face there, a regular customer.

The psychiatrist I saw at Newton-Wellesley last month was the one who'd lost most of his family in the Holocaust. He'd admonished me to "stay alive so you can tell."

Those words are with me now. When the tears stop, I look over at Dr. Grant.

"I need to finish what I've started," I say. "I need to tell someone in the church who has the authority to stop my father."

I wipe my face with my hands, push back my hair, and sit up a little straighter on the couch. I don't know where my resolve comes from. Suddenly I remember the first time I sang a solo in church. I was five. My knees knocked together, my voice cracked and wavered, my lips shivered. "Tell me the stories of Jesus," I sang, "I want to hear." Not long after that, I begged my father for a piano. I wanted to make music again, but was afraid to open my mouth.

Somewhere inside there must be a part of me who wants to live, wants to heal, wants to open her mouth and sing.

It's one week before my scheduled discharge. I'm sitting in my social worker's office, talking on the phone to Michael Robertson, director of pastoral relations at the National Association of Congregational Churches. Judy, my social worker, is standing by. I've just told my story.

"I can appreciate the turmoil." The words are sympathetic. The voice is not. "But at this point, what you are saying is nothing but hearsay."

I swallow hard.

"We don't have ecclesiastical powers—we advise congregations about their pastors, but what you are saying would require substantiation."

"My father has sent out dozens of dossiers over the years with decreasing numbers of children—four, then three, then two. He had five children." I'm shaking. I take a deep breath. "Both of my brothers committed suicide—my father lied about that, he has another daughter who says her mother left the marriage because of physical abuse—he's lied about that, and I am in the hospital trying to find a safe way to live with what I know happened."

"If information that's germane to a minister's ability to function is left off a dossier we would certainly pass that along, but we need proper documentation."

"What documents do you need? My brothers' death certificates? The false obituary my father put in the papers? My half-sister's birth certificate?"

"That would be helpful," he says. "After all, everyone is innocent until proven guilty."

"Who's on trial here?" I say, knowing I am. Judy puts a hand on my shoulder.

"Let me tell you what you're up against." I hear a long sigh. He's been down this road before. "Even with verifiable evidence, the church will be reluctant to believe your story."

I wait.

"Two years ago, we had a situation similar to yours which was substantiated by two daughters of one of our ministers. They claimed their father had raped both of them repeatedly throughout their lives. We notified the congregation. They did nothing. The situation erupted a year later with a civil suit. The minister was convicted. Only then did the church fire him."

"So what you're saying is I would have to file a civil suit in order to be taken seriously by the church?"

"If a civil suit takes place, that is fact. Everything else is hearsay. If you'd like, I'll give you the name of the chairman for the division of ministry."

He gives me the name, but I have stopped listening. I know that I don't have the strength to make another call, or to go through this again.

"Thank you," I say and hang up the phone.

I bury my face in my hands and cry.

Daddy is yawning behind the wheel. It's late at night. I am sitting next to him, smacking his thigh with my small hand to keep him awake. He is changing the channels on the radio, turning the dial. The static comes and goes. Since it is night, I am close to him. This is our secret time. I never sleep unless everyone else is asleep before me. He is the night driver. He, too, is awake in the night. But in the car, the lull of the engine makes him sleepy.

I want to stop patting his thigh. I want him to fall asleep, to see what he looks like, watch the lids of his eyes droop, then close, see the car careen slowly to the left, head on into the growl of an oncoming truck. But just before hitting the truck, and exploding into a fiery ball, I would grab the wheel and whip the car back into our lane. Daddy would wake up suddenly and yell, "Just what do you think you're doing?" and I would say calmly, "I'm saving your life."

Now I hear a tinkling of bells. It's the ice cream truck, parked outside the house in Baltimore. It's hot and sticky inside, we are fighting and drenched with sweat. For a moment the fighting stops. "Please, Daddy, can we get ice cream?" The bells tinkle again. His face softens. He reaches for his wallet and all four of us race out the front door and down the steps to meet the truck. The man in the white uniform and boat-shaped hat asks us what we'd like, and the colors we choose are orange—orange popsicle for Paul, orange creamsicle for David and me. Karen chooses a different colored popsicle, cherry. Daddy gets a fudgesicle and pays the man. Mommy stays inside for a brief moment of peace and quiet, which she says she likes better than ice cream. Paul, David, and I sit on the front steps, tearing off wrappers, sucking as fast as we can before the frozen treats melt and run down our fingers. Daddy, still standing, eats his fudgesicle fast. We are trying to keep up with him. Only Karen takes her time—she barely has the wrapper off by the time we're all finished.

Now I hear knocking. My best friend, Paula Renner, lives in the row house next door. Her bedroom is next to mine, and we've started knocking on the wall between us at night. Two knocks mean hello. Three knocks mean "Can you come over and play tomorrow?" Tonight Daddy is in my room. He is tucking me into bed, squeezing my feet through the sheets, which I like. I don't know if he will come back and wake me up later, which I don't like. Just then Paula knocks twice. Daddy stops. I freeze. Without a word, Daddy rises, makes a fist, and slams it hard into the wall, twice. Silence. "You'd better tell that Renner girl to stop knocking on our wall or I'll go over there and give her a piece of my mind." After he leaves there are three faint knocks, which I don't return. Daddy doesn't come back to wake me up later.

The next day at breakfast Daddy is quiet. I run over to Paula's to tell her he caught us and we have to stop. That night Daddy doesn't come back in my room to wake me up. Not the next night or the next or the next. He doesn't come into my room anymore at night, except now and then to tuck me in.

Sometimes I wonder what I have done wrong. I am six. My hair is changing from blonde to light brown, and Daddy doesn't call me his little blonde girl anymore. Once I was special. Now I'm not.

But at school I start piano lessons. I promise not to tell anyone about all those times when Daddy came to see me at night. Then one morning I wake up, run down the stairs and the piano is really there, all shiny and new, the white keys grinning like teeth. I don't have to practice at the church anymore. I am free.

When I play the piano I am still special. Daddy leaves me alone. Sometimes I wonder if the sounds I am making are like the bells on the ice cream truck and if, if I get good enough, he will never hurt me again. Like the Bible story we read in Sunday school where King Saul asks David to play on the harp to drive the evil demons away, I want to believe that's what happens when I play the piano.

Each night I get down on my knees and thank God for the piano, and pray that Daddy will not come in my room to wake me up. Since Paula knocked on the wall the last time and Daddy bought me the piano, he doesn't come anymore, so I believe God answers my prayers.

• • •

I am thinking about God—how I used to pray. I have this clear memory of believing in God, even when I was little and all the bad things with my father were happening. For so many years I prayed. Not in church, but out under the sky, especially at night, lying in the grass looking at the stars. I stopped praying after Paul died, after hearing my father say at his funeral, "the Lord giveth and the Lord taketh away."

Remembering my father in church brings back the phone call, and I am fully in the present. Michael Robertson doesn't seem to believe me, or doesn't want to, but since telling someone who is part of the church the secrets that I've kept all of my life, I have this new feeling about God. The thing that's kept me spiritually alone all of these years was somehow equating God with my father's church, and most of all, with my father. After hearing how the church responded to the minister's daughters who were raped, I see that God is not the church, God is not the National Association of Congregational Churches, and God is certainly not my father. At least not my biological father.

In Sunday school we used to sing "Jesus loves the little children, all the children of the world." It listed the colors, "red and yellow, black and white." For some reason I never felt I was on the list. I'd sing it as loud as I could, so that God would hear my voice, and I'd look over at the mural of Jesus gathering the children into his loving arms and wish I could be one of them.

For some reason, it feels possible now. I see us all gathered into these loving arms—my brothers, my sisters, and me.

I open my eyes and there is Judy, still waiting.

"I'm ready to go home now," I say.

She looks at me a bit skeptically. "After a phone call like that?"

I reach down inside myself for anything I might be missing. The gas tank reads empty.

"Well, I have one more week before discharge. If I'm going to fall apart again, I'll try to do it soon."

Judy smiles, but her eyes are still frowning. It reminds me of the face my mother used to wear—a strained smile when she was clearly upset.

"You'd better get going or you'll be late for your next group."

I miss my next group entirely, and spend the hour lying on my bed staring at the pictures I've taped to the wall: Meri and Eric and their little ones, Benji and Jen, plus a few crayon drawings of Jen's—a snake curving its way up through water with flowers hanging upside down; a photo of my sister Karen and her husband, Dave, with their arms wrapped around each other; another of my half-sister, Joanne, with her arm around me standing in the parking lot of the bus station in Milwaukee; one of Luci and me in our running shorts, numbers still pinned to our chests from our last 10K, another of us posing next to our dogs; several photos of my golden retriever, Nicky, swimming through waves at Martha's Vineyard and rolling in the sand afterward; and cards, letters, and postcards stuck up everywhere so I can read the "I love you's" whenever I need to. I'm homesick.

The one group I attend today is the group I've avoided for the whole month I've been in the hospital: Source, a spiritual resource group. The leader, Kathleen Adams, is the same woman who runs the journal group. She is trying to help us imagine God in whatever way we can, knowing that each of us has felt in her own way that if there ever were a God, He turned his back a long time ago.

At first, I feel alone and out of place. Kathleen asks us to find a word that means God to us. I have always felt closest to God in a wordless way. When I hear music—a string quartet, a bird's song, the lap of the ocean against the shore, I've felt God there. When I look at the sunset in all its striations of color, or the shower of stars at night, I've felt God there. But we are only allowed to write one word.

The word I write is *truth*. I do believe that God is truth, I say, and that someday the truth will be clear for all of us, the way the full moon makes a dark night clear, and the way the dawn comes clearly day after day.

Sarah, who's been going to AA meetings for twenty-five years, says "higherpower" as if it's one word. Sherry says "woman." She says "For sure God is a woman."

Alice, the blind woman, says, "comfort." To her, that is what God is. I envy her. I cannot say comfort and have it mean God.

Kathleen asks us to write about what we wish God meant to us. I write out a part of the Twenty-third Psalm I memorized when I was five: "Yea, though I walk through the valley of the shadow of death—" but I cannot write the part about the rod and the staff that comfort me because they don't.

Instead, I write what is true for me:

"Though I walk through the valley of the shadow of death, I don't have to stay. Soon I'll be walking out of here. I will probably fear everything. God will go with me. But my dog and my piano will comfort me."

III. NOVEMBER 1982–
JULY 1983/AUGUST 1992

NOVEMBER 1982–FEBRUARY 1983, BOSTON

THE LETTER ARRIVED today. My father has finally broken his long silence, and is demanding mine. He tells me I have done him a terrible injustice. How dare I insist that my memory of my childhood days in Baltimore is better than his, he asks. "If it had been a good memory, okay—but no, it was an alleged incident of a beating that I administered to you, Paul, and David that would make me guilty of flagrant child abuse!"

I remember the incident. I remember the den in the Baltimore house. It was just off the kitchen, but once the door was closed, my mother and sister were in another country. I remember the pine paneling. I used to pretend I could disappear into the knot holes. I remember lining up there next to my brothers, each of us dropping our pants, bending over, waiting, waiting. I remember hearing my father's belt snap across bare flesh once, then twice, then wishing I couldn't count. My brothers were braver than I. First Paul, who could go the longest without crying, who made it all the way to seven, then David, who wanted so badly to be as brave as Paul, but cried after five.

I am there now, tensing my butt and promising myself I won't cry, but after three I can't hold it back. I am the girl. I am weaker. My punishment is lighter. But also, there is the promised piano. If I say I'm sorry, if I don't talk back or tell anyone what goes on in our house, my father will buy me the piano. There, I can make all the sounds I want. I can cry out with my hands and no one will know it is animal pain coming out as music.

Now I am paid to make these sounds. I wish I could find the words for this pain. Not the music, but the words. The words that Paul could never speak, the words that David can only speak when he is watching his world fly apart, when he is locked up tight. The words that I can only utter as music.

My father is clear in his letter. "It was the insistence on your part that this alleged incident was *fact* that caused me to say, 'I hope you never have any children of your own . . . you will never be free to be a mother.'" He has always known the tender places, the places to wound.

My choices are clear, too. I can hang on to the memories that David spoke of while he was in the hospital, the memories that I confirmed to him in my letter. But believing my own memories, my own shared history with my brothers will cost me. My father says it will "cost you the beautiful relationship of love and affirmation that you have always known from your father and mother."

I can take it all back, say I made it up, say that David made it up, too. I can say I'm sorry for the thousandth time. I hear my mother's words. They are the same words she has always said: "Apologize to your father so I can have peace." I have always apologized through clenched teeth for saying the thing my father didn't want to hear. We all have. "You'd better apologize, Lindy," Paul used to say, "or you'll really get it." He'd quote from scriptures, put God's stamp on it. "Honor your father and mother so your days will be long on the earth," he'd say. Then he would laugh.

Right now, sitting at my piano, I just want to be with Paul. "Cheer up, Lindy," he'd say, and hug me sideways with one arm around my shoulder. He'd sit right next to me on the piano bench and sing Broadway tunes while I played the accompaniments. He'd played parts in the musicals *Oliver* and *The King and* I in high school, and I was his built-in rehearsal accompanist. He'd sing "Consider yourself part of the furniture," then he'd laugh and hug me with just his left arm. It's funny the way he'd give those one-armed hugs. A couple of years before he died he'd cut off his right index finger on the blade of a power rake. After that, it was as if he could only hug with his good arm, the one with five fingers at the end of it.

When I think of the cut-off finger, the way he saved it in a jar for a while, I wonder if that's when Paul first started to disappear. First one digit, and eventually the rest of him.

If I apologize, my father will let me back in. We will be one big, unhappy family again. I might lose my mind, but I won't lose my parents. It's a short trip to the edge of the cliff.

With Paul dead and David gone crazy, I'm not sure what's keeping me on higher ground.

In the time I am waiting to make up my mind about the letter, and whether to apologize or not, I try to practice. Liszt, *Paganini* Etude, no. 6. Rushing again. Each variation gathers speed. By the time I reach the sixth variation, con brio, the one with the octaves in both hands starting at opposite ends of the keyboard, the octaves are flying out of control. When my hands meet in the middle of the keyboard, and I'm preparing to make the turn back down with descending octaves, the notes are too close together, my hands moving too fast. No direction, pure speed, a cacophony of sound.

I have a lesson with Leonard Shure that is mostly lecture. He stops me before I finish playing the Liszt. He leaves the room to smoke a cigarette, returns to his chair beside the piano, and tells me what I already know.

"My dear, you are not involved in the music. You are somewhere else. Your fingers go without you, like a riderless horse."

"I'm sorry, " I say. It comes out so easily with him.

"You have to have a purpose when you practice. Don't just play notes. You have to have something to say."

What is it I'm trying to say with the music? What is it that can't be said with words?

On Sundays, Dan and I attend a Quaker meeting, one gift from Dr. Thomas that we've kept. The silent meeting is my only formal connection to God. There is no music. There is no minister. There are only people breathing together, praying or waiting for the Holy Spirit to move them.

Here, I'm not exposed week after week to the man in the pulpit who stands between me and God, between me and forgiveness. I am not exposed to the pain of remembering my father's words. There is no stained glass, only plain windows that let in the sunlight. There are no pews, only long benches with spindle backs that are turned toward the center facing each other. There is no altar, no cross, just plain white walls and a bare wooden floor. And there is the silence, which comforts me. At the end of the hour a woman speaks, then a man.

In my father's church, he always had the final word. At the end of each week, on the day after the beatings, he offered absolution. We could ask our Father in heaven through our earthly father, to forgive us our sins. "Our Father who art in Heaven," we'd begin. But as long as our father was leading it, the words seemed tainted.

When my father delivered the eulogy at my brother Paul's funeral, I didn't hear most of the words. But I remember the sound of his voice, invincible, lofty, as if he were delivering the Sunday sermon. I heard no pain or remorse in his voice, only the steady rendering of my brother's achievements—honor student, National Merit Scholar, successful businessman, witness for Christ. I was listening for something, a waver in his voice, a choked-back sob, a catch in his breath, anything that would prove he was more a father losing a son than a minister addressing his congregation. There, at the front of the sanctuary, lay my brother in his coffin. Above him, in the pulpit, stood my father in his robes.

We rode to the cemetery in silence. I watched the back of the hearse the whole time as if I were holding my brother's flower-strewn coffin in place with my eyes. When his coffin was lowered into the ground, my father uttered the final words over his dead son. His voice never cracked, not once.

My father wants the final word again. In his letter to me he writes, "It is necessary to reconstruct memory tapes." The last sentence is written in King James's English. "Would to God the former days could be restored."

If I apologize to my father, the former days will be restored.

If I hand over my memories, he will erase them.

I can count on one hand the number of people with whom I'm comfortable sharing eighty-eight keys. My sister, Karen, although we have the most arguments over territory—her hands are just one note larger than mine and sometimes she'll spread them further than she needs to just to aggravate me. My closest friend from Vail, Maro, who helped me rewrite a Scarlatti Sonata and a Bach Gigue into a virtual relay race around the piano, the keyboard serving as baton, the point being never to drop a beat. And Mil, my mother-in-law and former piano teacher, with whom I am playing duets on this old Chickering grand at the October Country Inn.

Since this is the one inn where Dan and I were both happy at the same time, the one that saved our bike vacation from total disaster, we decided to bring Dan's folks here for Christmas.

We actually spent Christmas day with Eric and Meri— wore the matching reindeer aprons they gave us, stuffed our first turkey together, and served the feast on the red plates and embroidered holly placemats Dan's grandmother gave us. We picked up Dan's folks at the airport Christmas night. Mil and Fil spoiled me with expensive clothes. This year it was a dark green cashmere suit with red piping around the edges and a soft red leather bag that opened like an envelope.

"To go with those red shoes you wore in Washington," Mil said.

I ran my fingers over the soft leather bag, and nodded without looking up.

We drove to Vermont the next day.

My parents are finally speaking to me, even though I didn't apologize. I called on Christmas day, and they said they hadn't opened their gifts yet. I labored for hours remaking a robe for my mother—sewing remnants of lace from an old dressing gown around the neck and cuffs of a new robe. I suppose it's a bit like putting new wine into old skins, but I wanted to somehow weave the past into the present, hoping she'd recognize it. I thanked them for our gifts, but the conversation was so strained that my mouth hurt from trying to smile. The smile was my Christmas gift to my mother who said, "You don't sound very cheery, dear." My sister, Karen, talked to me, too. We talked about everything but our brother, David. Then there was nothing left to say.

After David was released from the hospital in Florida, he lost his job and moved to Connecticut to live with Vickie's parents. He's unemployed, severely depressed, and taking whatever he has left of Thorazine. He's going to run out soon, but he refuses to see a psychiatrist. I sent him a list of shrinks my therapist recommended. My father sent him a list of headhunters. "All David needs is a new job," he said. David threw out the list of shrinks and kept the headhunters.

He talks to me now, but mostly in monosyllables. When I called on Christmas, he thanked me for his gift and for the book I sent little Dave, Shel Silverstein's *Where the Sidewalk Ends*. While I was talking to Vickie, I heard him laugh at one of the poems he was reading to little Dave: "Mama said I'd lose my head if it wasn't fastened on/ and the other day it wasn't/ 'cause while playing with a cousin/ it fell off and rolled away and now it's gone . . ." I wondered what he was thinking when he read that poem. For a split second, it felt like my old brother was back.

I could hear little Dave's voice afterward, "where the sidewalk ends," then a page turn, "where the sidewalk ENDS," another page flip, "where the *sidewalk ends*." He's six years old, just learning to read, and he reads everything, even if it's the same thing, over and over again, sounding out words. A whole new world is opening up for him while the rest of his world is falling apart. I think I'll send him books every Christmas for the rest of his life.

My brother David apologized for not sending Dan and me gifts. There was pain in his voice. He's always been a big gift-giver. When I was little, he bought me my first Barbie doll with money he'd earned on a paper route. He was trying to replace the doll my cousin Patricia had brought me from France, which had blue eyes that opened and closed and braided gold hair, real hair. That was the doll David said he'd "fixed" by taking the eyes out. When I woke up and saw the empty sockets, I cried. He promised to get me another doll.

When I was twelve, David bought me my very first bra. My mother didn't notice that my small nipples were beginning to stick out like pencil erasers. David did, and at first he made fun of them, but then under the Christmas tree I found the box and it said "From Santa" in his handwriting. He must have gone right into the girls' underwear section of Fowler's Department Store. I was embarrassed but secretly grateful.

In high school, he drove me from Cheyenne to Denver, took me to a leather shop at Cinderella City, and bought me my first real leather coat, purple suede with gold snaps. I kept the coat until my sister, Karen, who'd outgrown me by two inches, wore it, and ripped the arms out of the seams. She was always Dave's "pet" sister, and probably felt like the coat should have been hers anyway.

After he joined the Navy and went to Vietnam, David's gifts got more exotic—raw silk from Thailand, and a lacquered wooden jewelry box with tiny drawers and a little window. When you lifted the lid you could see a kimono-clad doll with a parasol rock back and forth in a rickshaw just inside the window. That jewelry box is one of the only things I've kept from growing up—that, and the raw silk, once made into a prom gown and later into a long flowing skirt that I now wear for chamber music concerts.

I told David that I didn't care about not getting Christmas gifts this year.

"There's only one thing I want from you anyway, and it doesn't cost anything."

"Yeah, right," he said. "Like what?"

"I just want you to promise that you'll never do what Paul did."

"Don't worry about it—"

"Well, I want you to promise. That's all I want."

"I would never do that."

"Promise?"

"You got it."

That was the best Christmas gift I got.

I'm sitting at this old grand piano with Mil, performing Schubert's Fantasy in F minor for four hands. The opening is so simple—a broken F-minor chord that Mil plays with such absolute stillness that when I enter with the repeated Cs moving to F and back, outlining the haunting open fifth of the melody, it's like dipping my fingers into a calm, transparent pool of water. The music stays submerged until the fast dance section in 3/4 time, then the opening theme returns, bursts into the grand fugue, and returns one last time at the finale. I love playing this part with Mil—she has huge hands for such a tiny person—and a big resonant sound that makes the piano rumble like a tremor under the earth. When the fugue dies down there is a measure of silence, and the calm opening F-minor chord returns. It is the final breath, then, in a few short measures, the music dies.

Finally, my brother David wants to see me. I don't know what opened the door. Maybe since my mind is on other things, it is safe for him to see me now. My schedule is crazy: two solo recitals, one in two weeks; four chamber music concerts, the first next week; three concerto performances, one next month and two with the Boston Pops (luckily, the same concerto); and a new interdisciplinary course (Music, Art, and Drama) that I agreed to team-teach at Northeastern. I'm more prepared for the concerts and teaching than I am for this visit.

The drive from Boston to Stratford, Connecticut, feels long. Luckily, Dan is driving. I am studying the score for the Mozart concerto I'm about to play for Shure, trying to fight fear with fear.

It is a shock to see David. My handsome brother, who had all of my girlfriends after him in high school, who used to turn heads without even summoning a smile, who proudly posed naked from the waist up for photos sent home during Vietnam, has gotten fat. I don't know if it's the Thorazine, the immobility of his days, or his mother-in-law's cooking. There's no accounting for the rest of the changes—his usually trimmed beard is scraggly, his thick brown hair, which he used to spend hours combing, falls loosely down the base of his neck. He smokes endless Marlboros—reds, the kind that kill you faster. His brown eyes are listless, underlined with dark crescent moons. He barely talks.

He lets me walk with him alone, up the short street from his in-laws' house, to buy more cigarettes. He lets me lace my arm through his, and for those minutes while we walk, we are brother and sister again, and that link is what keeps me from running away. That, and the memory that when I ran away at sixteen, David was the one who drove from Cheyenne down to the Sangre de Cristo Mountains in Colorado to find me.

There are so many things I want to say—"Get help, please!" I mutter, knowing that he won't, and he answers by blowing smoke in my face. It's the long exhales that bother me, as if he is letting out a little more life with every breath.

He's wearing the same gold down jacket he's owned since high school, the one he used to wear skiing. We used to call him the Michelin Man. I start to say it, but my lips stay pursed for the *m*. I breathe through my nose. It's not the jacket. How can a man grow larger and yet seem so diminished at the same time?

After one "please get help" I am silent. I cling to what he is offering—his arm.

What breaks me up is watching my brother's son, little Dave. He runs around like a toy train on a circular track, only slowing to approach his father with the caution of someone who's been stung by bees too many times, but still wants the honey. If there were ever a time I wish my brother would put down his cigarette, it is when his seven-year-old son is standing next to him, offering a book, a record, or tape. My brother waves him away with the burning cigarette dangling from his fingers—"Not now, kiddo," he says, then with a bit of sarcasm in his voice, "can't you see I'm busy?"

Vickie is sitting with David, Dan, and me at the kitchen table in her parents' house. She looks haggard—her blonde hair hangs limply over her shoulders—and I wonder how long she can handle the strain of working at a nursing home, nursing my brother through his depression, and caring for little Dave.

"Why don't you play with your son?" she says. "You're not doing anything and he knows it."

My brother continues to smoke. I feel my stomach twist like the wet towel my brother used to wring between two hands and snap. I wish he would do that now. Something, anything, but sit there and smoke.

Flossie, Vickie's mother, is taking a dish of lasagne out of the oven. She is the angel of this house, taking care of her daughter, her grandson, and her son-in-law as if all three were her children. My brother is closer to her than he is to our mother. Flossie is the one person he really talks to, when he talks.

"Will somebody set the table?" she asks.

I jump to my feet, anxious to escape my own helplessness, and nod to Dan.

Dan picks up the cue. He sits down on the floor with little Dave listening to the record. It's Pink Floyd, "Daddy's record," little Dave says. I watch my husband and see that someday he will be a good father, the kind of father my brother cannot be right now. I watch my brother watch Dan, and I know he knows it, too.

On the drive home, Dan is quiet. I think I am losing him. He is tired of my family, tired of my music, and unhappy in his job. He doesn't say any of that out loud, but it's there. I hear it sideways. When his mother calls and asks him about my upcoming performances, he says "ask her yourself" and hands me the phone. Later, he complains that his mother is never interested in *his* work. I tell him she just doesn't understand banking, and needs more than one-word answers. He says, at the moment, one-word answers are what he has to offer, and if she spent a little less time talking about music and a little more time listening to him talk about banking, she might learn something. He is angry, so angry, but it is not just about my music. It's about his mother's interest in my music.

It's one month until my first performance of the Mozart Concerto in A (K. 488), and Shure is still shouting about the direction of each phrase. I am impatient to get through the whole concerto and we are still stuck on the first movement, exposition. He is impatient that I'm not getting the musical direction, and although he's just heard me play the whole first movement without shouting, "No, no, *no!*" he has lit enough cigarettes to let me know what he thinks.

"Well, my dear, you can play it that way if you like." He shakes out another cigarette, lights it.

"What way?" I ask. I'm not afraid to talk back to him. I just can't stand waiting for the criticism.

"Well, it's very pretty the way you play it." From Leonard Shure, this is not a compliment.

I wait, stare at the keys, shifting figure and ground. What if the black keys were the main ones and the white keys were just background? What if my way is right and his way is wrong?

"But it's bloodless." He takes another drag on his cigarette. "Now, if you want to breathe real life into the music that's another matter."

As the smoke billows around me I feel a giant sucking inside, like quicksand. Give it up, just give it all up, the voice inside me says. You don't have it in you to do this. It's too hard.

Shure has just put out his cigarette, which is the signal to get to work. I want to say, "Listen, Mr. Shure, my husband hates my music, my brother is depressed and suicidal, and I don't give a damn about breathing life into this dead concerto, so if you'll just excuse me, I think I'll go home and sleep for a month."

Instead, I restart the opening solo.

"No, no, *no!*" he shouts, waving his hands in front of him as if he is shooing away flies. "The first four bars come *from* the one!" he shouts. "The last two bars *fall!*"

I stare at the score in front of me. It is the full orchestral score, so the piano part is sandwiched in between all the orchestra parts. The little black dots are swimming on the page. I know what sound each dot represents: pitch, duration, timbre, dynamic, but I still don't understand the direction. Shure pencils in an arrow, pointed over the first four bars toward the downbeat. For the life of me I don't know what it means. I have studied with this man for a year now, imitated his playing of every phrase, but I realize now that I don't understand how he got there. I have two choices: I can leave this lesson with a pale imitation of the way Shure plays, or try to understand the way he thinks. If I tell him I don't understand, I run the risk of igniting his wrath, but since I'm getting that anyway, I might as well learn something.

"Mr. Shure, what do you mean when you say the first four bars come *from* the one? I don't get it."

I brace for the storm.

Instead, Shure's face softens.

"You mean you've been studying with me all of this time and you don't get it?"

"Right."

"What's not to get?"

"Well, I hear your playing, and I know it's the way this phrase should sound, but I look at the score and I don't know how you got there."

Shure sighs heavily, pushes his chair away from the piano.

"All right, then, get up."

Here it comes. He's going to ask me to leave. I stand up, start to gather my music.

"No, no," he says, waving his hands, "leave that there. Stand over here, in front of the fireplace."

I walk out into the middle of Shure's living room, relieved to be away from the piano, but unsure of myself. I wonder if he's going to ask me to dance. I don't know how to partner dance, and I would be so embarrassed to dance with Shure. He stands, rather tall in front of me, and I notice the narrow cut of his jeans. He's a smart dresser for a man in his seventies, a handsome, imposing figure. He moves in beside me and suddenly I'm aware of his cologne. Feeling him this close to me throws me a little off balance. It reminds me of my father, how relieved I was when he stopped yelling, how scary it was to stand close to him.

"Now, take one step forward, like this." Shure steps forward with his right foot. I step forward. "Now step back onto your left foot." He rocks back and forth between the foot in front and the foot behind. "Two points don't necessarily imply direction," he says, stepping from his left foot onto his right, "but if I take a third step," he takes another step forward with his left foot, "now I have a direction."

I take another step forward with my left foot.

"There," Shure points to my feet. "That's commitment. You've committed to a direction. That's what I want you to do with the music."

Shure heads back to the piano. I follow. He sits down, looks up at the score, and plays an E followed by a C-sharp.

"By themselves, these two notes don't have a direction." He plays D.

"Now they do. If I make a slight crescendo toward the D, the direction is toward the downbeat of the second bar." Shure plays. "If I make a slight decrescendo in the slur between the first two notes going to D, keep the sound level through the second bar, then fall or decrescendo toward the third and fourth bar, the musical direction is coming from the first beat of the phrase—from the one."

I stand behind Shure, listening, looking over his shoulder at the score. For the first time, the direction is clear. I am able to connect it with what other teachers have called by different names. In college, Margie May used to write "lead this" when she wanted the musical direction to go toward the downbeat, and "easy" when she wanted it to fall away. At the New England Conservatory, Patricia Zander would ask, "Where is it going?" letting you make the discovery by playing the phrase. In Switzerland, at Ernen Musikdorf, Gyorgy Sebok would say "play this phrase as if you are moving toward the future," or "play this as if you are moving away from the past." It sounds like the same thing, at last I understand. "Coming from the one" is the same musical direction as "moving away from the past."

After the lesson, sitting at my piano, I study every phrase to see if I can determine the direction for myself. "Is this moving toward the one or away from it?" I ask myself. "Away from the past or toward the future?" Somewhere in the development section of the first movement of the Mozart, it occurs to me that this is what the music itself is doing—moving me from my past toward my future. Without the music, there would only be the quicksand, the constant sucking away from the present, away from my life.

A letter arrives today from my father. It's a six-page reply to the letter I wrote him back in November, the one where I didn't apologize. He answers my questions about Baltimore, and offers to send the photos I asked for, the ones of me as a little blonde girl. It's the time in my life when he says I was the happiest. I have no memory of that time except for the beatings, and coming home to the new piano he bought me. I remember the blonde girl in the photographs, but I don't remember what it was like to be her.

Musicians create their own time, outside linear time, yet still within it. This has always been the hardest part for me. I feel the clock or the metronome ticking, and I am driven to get to the next beat. I often feel as if someone is standing behind me while I play, breathing down my neck, waiting for me to hurry up and finish. It may have to do with the temporary safety I used to feel at the piano, never knowing when my time would be up.

I've always had trouble breathing—not just in music, but in life. The summer after my brother Paul died I was waiting tables at the Old San Francisco Steak House in Dallas, watching the girl on the red swing fly through the air above the bar, spinning and spinning. I thought of my brother dangling from the rope, his body suspended in midair. Oh, how I wanted the rope to break and his thin body to come tumbling down. I was carrying a huge tray with a very expensive bottle of wine, balancing the tray on my shoulder, when suddenly I couldn't breathe. I passed out just before delivering the wine to my table, heard the shattering glass, and came to in my boss's office calling "Paul, Paul," between breaths. Since my boss's name was Paul, he'd answered "What, what?" before holding a paper bag to my mouth and ordering me to breathe into it.

At this morning's rehearsal in Symphony Hall, I missed my first entrance. Big memory slip. Hearing the opening tutti of the Mozart, the sound of that great orchestra surrounding me, I forgot who I was or what I was there to do. I was sitting on stage at Alfred Brendel's old Steinway. I chose it for its rich, creamy resonance, and because the spirit of the music probably still lives there. Brendel must have performed this Mozart concerto hundreds of times.

Still, once I got over the memory slip and began playing, it was like skating on black ice, smooth and glassy, no bumps, but still skating too fast. Now that I understand the direction of every phrase, I just want to get to the end, as if the destination were more important than the journey. Sometimes I am there before the orchestra. Martha Babcock, whose ears I've come to trust, came up to me after the rehearsal and patted me on the back. "It's beautiful," she said, "but give it a little more room—more poise."

As much as I rushed, Harry Ellis Dickson slowed down. The third movement is marked "presto." I strained to move forward and did. But Harry got slower, and each phrase was a tug of war. Toward the end of the Rondo, I got help from the clarinet section. Someone yelled, "It's too slow, Harry!" and the tempo sped up.

It's not just the difference in metabolism between Harry and me that's the problem. I've always rushed. And every teacher I've ever studied with has looked for a way to slow me down.

"Practice as if you have more time," Shure said a week ago, "as if you had months, not days to prepare."

On the way home from Symphony Hall, I realize I have the whole day to stretch out, study the score, sleep, take a bath. Dan is at work, and although my parents flew into Boston for the concert, they drove first to Connecticut to see David, Vickie, and little Dave. I asked them to wait until just before the concert to arrive. I knew I needed the time to practice.

At home, I listen to the tape of the rehearsal, and realize that it went better than I had thought, that a new kind of music-making is coming out of me. It is less showy, more well-informed. Instead of going for extremes in dynamics, I am actually containing my sound within a certain range, and expressing subtle nuances that I might not have even heard a year ago. The problem tonight will be how to make the Pops audience hear them, how to get them to quiet down enough to hear the opening solo.

I mark all of the parts that still need work. I sit down at the piano and begin practicing my first entrance when I hear the hum of a large automobile in the driveway. I look out the window and immediately recognize my parents' yellow Oldsmobile, Wisconsin plates. My mother is at the door first.

"Hi, Mom," I say, looking at my watch. It's noon.

"Hello, dear." She reaches for a hug. I give it.

My father slams the car door and walks up the steps to the deck. He hugs me so hard I feel all the breath squeezed out of me. He tries to kiss me. I turn my head.

"You don't seem very happy to see us," my mother says.

"Well, you're only about seven hours early."

My mother steps back. Guilt tightens like a noose around my neck. I swallow my anger and ask about their visit with David.

"He wasn't in a very good mood, so we left early."

I get it. Concert pianist daughter wins out over paranoid schizophrenic son. I am living, performing proof that they are good parents. David is not. I don't know if I'm more angry because my parents have arrived on my doorstep seven hours ahead of schedule or because they've abandoned my brother again.

I apologize for having nothing to give them for lunch. My mother offers to grocery shop. I make a list a mile long. Although she can drive herself, my mother asks my father to drive her. I'm grateful.

As soon as the car pulls out of the driveway I open the score for the Mozart and review my penciled notes, which are the same throughout: "Wait—hold back—stretch—more time—breathe!" I play the opening solo and stop. My hands are shaking a bit. I've been trying so hard not to think about David, how he is doing, what he is doing since quitting the job he'd just started, what he is thinking since Mom and Dad left early, whether he hates me for being the momentary family star. I can't keep the thoughts back. I open the notebook that's near the piano and write.

Family star. It's the spot Paul used to occupy. Whatever David tried, everyone compared him to Paul: teachers, friends, and especially our father. When David became a National Merit Scholar, it was no big deal because Paul had already done it. The summer after David graduated from high school, he sold Bibles door to door because Paul had done it. Paul had just finished rebuilding a Volkswagen engine for Sandi when David started working on his Volkswagen.

"Why don't you wait until your brother comes home," Dad said. "He can help you with that."

David threw the wrench across the garage.

If Paul's achievements cast a long shadow, his death cast an even longer one. I know David thinks about that, though he never talked about it. Not until last fall when he ended up in the hospital. That was right after he wrote me the letter of congratulations for my concerts.

I tell myself it wasn't my fault, and that sabotaging this concert is not going to help put my brother's life back together. I tell myself that we have the same father and we have the same anger—the self-destructive kind. I tell myself that the same father who beat the shit out of us, who made us swear we wouldn't tell anyone, did some good things, too. He bought me a piano and he paid for my lessons. For that, I think I owe him this concert. And the thought that I owe him this concert makes me want to throw it.

But then I think about the conductors I've worked with who are old enough to be my father and fifty times more accomplished than he. Instead of conducting my every move, they conduct the music. They don't own me. They don't own the music. Nobody does. Not the conductor, not the orchestra, not the audience, not even the composer, who is dead after all. How can I feel that my father owns my music?

If I sabotage this concert, I'll still believe my father owns my music. I might as well let him pen his initials into the score. I'm getting paid to do this concert. If I play well, maybe I'll own a little more of myself. Maybe I'll even autograph a few programs, send one to my brother.

My parents don't return for two hours. Dan comes home early from work, and keeps my parents occupied while I sleep, take a bath, and try to figure out what to wear. Dan's grandmother bought me a new gown, magenta taffeta, but I am afraid it will make noise during the slow movement—all those *pianissimos*. I opt for something simple—the ice-pink silk I wore for all of my solo concerts this spring. It's noiseless, and the slit in the front makes it easy to pedal.

From my dressing room at Symphony Hall, I happen to catch a glimpse of my father racing across the street toward the hall. He gives a thumbs up signal, and I smile and wave, thinking it's for me. But then I look and see Dan at the stage door, returning his signal. Apparently, my father found a parking spot. I close the Levolor blinds, shut out the world, and slip into my pink silk gown. I sit down at the piano and open the full orchestra score of the Mozart, then map out all of the themes of the opening tutti—A, A1, B, B1, etc. The last theme before my entrance is marked D.

"Don't daydream," I tell myself.

I hear the hum of audience chatter that means intermission. The stage manager, Cleve, knocks on my dressing room door, tells me I'm next.

Symphony Hall is noisier than usual tonight. On stage I'm adjusting the knobs on the bench, Harry is standing very still at the podium, head bowed, baton held low. The audience is talking, laughing, and clinking glasses when someone in the woodwind section stands up and says "shh." After a few loud coughs, including one from my father, the orchestra begins the opening tutti.

At the end of the tutti the audience is calm, my mind is quiet, and, after the letter D, I forget myself, and remember only the music. There is still a slight tug-of-war here and there for the right tempo, me playing forward to the ends of phrases, Harry pulling the orchestra back. But finally, in the cadenza, where I can play as fast or as slow as I want while the orchestra waits, I feel utterly free, as if I've been momentarily released from the tyranny of someone else's beat. I begin the last trill before the orchestra's entrance, accelerate, and float to the end of the first movement.

In the slow movement, there is the stillness of a sleeping baby. I play the second theme more and more quietly until there is almost no sound. I hear my own breath, and feel that the audience breathes with me. A heartbeat before I play the return of the opening theme, there is a hush in the audience. It's as if there is only the quiet of this moment, and I am playing the opening nine notes for the very first time.

In the last movement I am the first horse out of the gate with the solo. I take off at a clip. The orchestra delivers a brisk answer with a squeak at the end of the phrase from the clarinets. Still, the orchestra is with me, and instead of slowing the ends of phrases while I rush, we are married to the beat. There is a kind of athletic exhilaration in the playing of this movement, a release from the tragic sadness of the second movement, and a buoyant race through Alberti basses to the finish line. When we get there, the audience bursts into applause. Maybe it's from relief that they don't have to be quiet any longer. This, after all, is the Boston Pops, and I have a feeling that this audience is more comfortable cheering for the Red Sox than for Mozart.

Backstage, John Williams, who is standing behind Harry Dickson, takes both of my hands. "Bravo," he says. "It was beautiful." I am so honored that he came, and so relieved that I didn't know he was there.

My mother is next in line. "Well, it wasn't as exciting as the Shostakovich," she says, hugging me, "but I'm still proud."

"I thought you hated Shostakovich," I whisper, knowing that whatever nuance I'd shaped in tonight's performance is lost on her.

"Well sure—when you were practicing it at home alone," she says. "It was much better with the orchestra."

Dan gives me a bouquet of white roses, and a kiss. While in his arms I hear my father's preaching voice.

"Was that John Williams?" he broadcasts as John heads up the backstage stairs.

I want to die right there, but I hug my father instead and whisper, "Yes, Dad, but please keep your voice down."

Alone in my dressing room, I change back into my civilian clothes. There are flowers all around me—yellow roses from my in-laws, a bouquet of irises, lilies, and roses from my sister and her husband, Dave, and more roses from my friend Maro, in Vail. I sink my nose into the yellow roses and feel the presence of friends and family who couldn't be here tonight.

And I feel the absence of both of my brothers, living and dead.

One of the orchestra members throws a party for me after the concert. Even with my parents there, I drink more champagne than I can handle. For the moment I want to ignore the rest of the concerts and auditions that crowd the months of May and June. I want to think up another occupation.

As a little girl, I used to love playing with my brothers' trucks. Some part of me still wants to operate a big piece of machinery—a crane, a forklift, some huge earth-moving machine. The piano is a big machine—the way the hammers and keys work is all very mechanical—and the strings have enough tension in them, that were they to burst, there would be enough force to explode a small building. But a piano doesn't affect lives in any tangible way. That's always bothered me. In college, I used to feel guilty about the number of hours I spent practicing instead of doing something that would save lives, or more important, the souls that inhabit them. Harry Dixon, an economics professor who was one of my surrogate fathers during college, used to listen to me complain about all the hours spent practicing when I could be doing something useful, become a missionary, perhaps. He'd say to me, "Don't become one of those Christians who's so heavenly minded they're no earthly good." I think he meant that practicing was probably a better use of my time than trying to convert the lost. Part of me wanted to believe that the music I made on earth would somehow *reach* the heavens, or at least tilt the ears of the listeners upward.

Still, there's this feeling of futility that comes over me after a concert, even one that's gone well, and I'm not sure that all the hours spent preparing weren't wasted when the performance is over in less than thirty minutes. It must be the way a chef feels after spending all day on a lavish feast only to watch it disappear in a few hungry minutes. What is the work that would make my life feel meaningful, that would make me jump out of bed in the morning, unable to sleep another minute for the excitement of the task ahead? If I were to become, say, a drawbridge operator, I would at least be saving lives every day—those in the cars going over the bridge and in the boats coming under.

My brother Paul used to tell a story where a drawbridge operator was God. There's a boat coming through with hundreds of people on it, he'd say, and the drawbridge operator sees his son playing in the gears. If he runs out to save his son, all the people in the boat will be killed. If he raises the drawbridge to let the boat through, all those people will live, but he will crush his son in the gears. God sacrifices his only son.

If I were the drawbridge operator, which would I choose? The decision, like which key to strike and with what kind of force, would have to be made in a split second. The sound would be piercing either way.

•   •   •

After my second performance of the Mozart concerto with Pops, which settled into a more comfortable marriage between piano and orchestra, I'm on a plane headed for Milwaukee. My parents are picking me up, driving me to Green Bay. They are moving again. This time into an apartment. They're getting rid of things that they've carried from house to house for years. I'm going there to pick up pieces of my past—old music, my wind-up metronome, high school and college yearbooks, family photos.

Right now there are so many missing pieces in my life. I'm hoping this trip will help fill them in. My father has promised me slides from Baltimore. There's a little blonde girl in those photos. They say she is me. I'd like to reclaim her, bring her home.

We're descending into Milwaukee. You can see the brewery stacks from the sky. I tasted my first beer here. I was nine. I had a friend, Julie, whose father ran the Schlitz brewery, and they served beer instead of milk to their kids.

My parents drive me from the airport to Wauwatosa, the section of Milwaukee where we lived for two years when I was eight and nine. I want to see the old houses. We drive past the old parsonage on Church Street, the Victorian house we moved into after the Baltimore row house. My father drives by slow enough for me to notice that the old falling down porch where I played endless games of Ping-Pong with my mother and brothers is missing, replaced by a built-on garage. I look up and see the third-floor window that was my safe place—a room off the bathroom where I painted with oils from a paint-by-number set, and fancied myself an artist. I loved that room. No one ever came up there, and the window looked out over the big apple tree with the tire swing in the backyard. I painted that scene over the one on the paint-by-number canvas.

We drive one street over to Ridge Court, where we'd moved to a newer parsonage after a year in the old one. I thought it was the fanciest house we'd ever had—a brick colonial with several sets of sliding glass doors. A mansion. It looks dwarfed now, plainer than I remember it. The church had bought the house from a real artist, and she left me her old easel in the basement, which became my windowless studio.

"Have you seen enough?" My father is drumming his fingers on the steering wheel, letting me know he's impatient to leave this town where he grew up.

I want to drive by the field where I played baseball with my brothers, walk up into the woods and see if the remains of our old fort is still there, the one that caved in and almost suffocated my brothers and me, but maybe it's better to leave some things to the imagination.

My parents' house in Green Bay is already stacked with boxes. Most of mine are in the basement. But when I open the music cabinet near the piano, and find many of my old music books missing, I look up at my father, who looks over at my mother.

"Karen has already taken hers," my mother says.

"What do you mean *hers*? Those books were mine first. I lent them to her."

"Now, don't get upset, dear. You've always had more than your sister. I just thought it would make sense to let her take some music first."

The old sibling rivalry wells up, for all the old reasons. I had to share the piano with her, share my music with her, share my bedroom with her. There was nothing that was either all hers or all mine. Even our parents got divided— Karen was Mom's daughter, and I was Dad's.

"I told your mother to let you pick out the music first," Dad says.

"It's okay, Dad," I say. But really they should have let us do it together. Then we could have scratched and clawed each other's eyes out.

What I really wish is that my sister and I could be friends. But I don't know if friendship with Karen is possible. My mother needs her too much to allow us to team up. And my father needs me.

After church on Sunday, I hear my mother whisper something to Karen in the kitchen, and overhear the end of it.

"Don't say anything about it to Linda."

I pretend not to hear, and walk into the living room, where my father is setting up the slide projector to show slides of Baltimore. Karen and her husband, Dave, sit next to me on the couch, and I feel like a third wheel. If Dan were here, we'd be four, just like we were growing up, and I wouldn't feel as alone. If our brother David were here, I'd still feel alone, because he and Karen have always taken the same side, whether in family arguments or on couches.

The slide show begins, and we laugh at the dowdy red brick row houses in Baltimore, and tell Dave about Madeline Murray O'Hare, the atheist who lived down the street from us who got school prayer abolished. Her son went to our grade school. Kids used to throw stones at him. We all laugh about that, until I realize we are laughing so mercilessly at someone's pain, a family tradition I never used to question.

A slide appears of the four of us sitting on the front steps of our Baltimore house. My mother is holding Karen, she must be one and a half, and I am five, sitting next to my brothers. I feel Karen stiffen looking at this slide.

"We look so depressed," she says, and for a moment, I think there might be some real connection between us.

"You don't know what it is to be depressed," my father says. "Your mother and I lived through the real Depression. You kids just don't know how good you had it."

I look at those slides and feel nothing. I don't know the little sad-faced girl with the curly blonde hair. She seldom looks into the camera—mostly her face is turned to the side or her eyes are looking down.

"Look at those blonde curls," my mother beams. "You were the apple of your father's eye."

I think of the apple I threw at a car from high up in a tree. It hit the driver in the head, and she got out of the car and started walking toward me, waving her fist and shouting. My friend Nancy and I jumped out of the tree, ran inside her house and hid. When the woman came to the door, I overheard my friend's mother say, "Oh no, that's our minister's daughter—she would never do anything like that." I must have been eight or nine. It was my first real awareness of getting away with sin.

The next slide is the one of David throwing the rock at my father, who is behind the camera. We've all seen this slide before and burst into laughter. But this time, knowing where David has been this past year, we are silent as stone. My father clicks by it to the next shot, Karen and Paul in the pool at Ghost Ranch in Abiquiu, New Mexico. Karen looks about two, and Paul must be nine. He is holding a ball and pointing to Karen where he's going to toss it. Her chubby little fingers are splayed above the water and she is squinting into the sun.

"I don't remember Paul ever playing with me," Karen says, and my father holds that shot on the screen a little longer. I look over and see Karen's eyes fill with tears. We've always been told that Paul and I were the ones who were close, and she and David. The narration doesn't always fit the pictures.

"Save that one, Dad," I say.

"But you're not in that one."

"I want a copy anyway. I don't have that many pictures of Paul as a kid. Karen, either."

My sister looks over at me wide-eyed. It's a start. Small, but a start.

After the slide show, Karen agrees to bring back the music she took so we can go through it together. We hug, and she holds on to me a little longer than usual.

The next morning, Mom makes buttermilk pancakes, the one thing I can always count on from her, and my father and I pile them on to our plates and linger over the last drop of coffee, postponing the final excavation of the basement boxes.

What fills in first are the missing pieces of my father's past. He opens the box I remember finding in the Cheyenne house—the one with World War II mementos. Paul, David, and I had stumbled on it in the laundry room, opened it, and pulled out a Nazi flag, a German tablecloth and napkins, two German bayonets, and a hand grenade before our father stormed into the laundry room, grabbed the things out of our hands, and shouted, "Don't you *ever* open this box again."

That is the box he is opening now. He hands me the folded ice-blue embroidered tablecloth and napkins.

"Want these?"

Dumbfounded, and still feeling guilty over the first Pandora episode, I finger the cloth and admire the fine needlework. The initials A.M. are embroidered in script on every napkin.

"Where did you get these?"

"Some bombed-out German house in Berlin."

I don't ask what happened to the inhabitants or why my father kept these. I am holding a piece of his past that he's never allowed any of us to touch. This is a delicate moment that could disappear with one wrong word. My father sifts through the layers of the box like an archaeologist—carefully digging, trying not to unsettle any of the fragile remains of another time. From under the Nazi flag, he pulls out a photo album, blows the dust off the cover and opens it to the first page.

Right off, I recognize my father's father—the stern man who died just after Paul was born, and my grandmother, but the way she looked before I knew her. A beautiful little blonde girl sits in my grandfather's lap, her head turned away from the camera. If it weren't for the clothes from the 1940s and Grandpa Cutting's presence, I might have mistaken it for a photograph of me in the Baltimore years—same sad eyes, same facial structure, same turning away from the man behind the camera.

"That's Joanne, isn't it?"

My father doesn't answer. He is staring at the photographs, lost in another time and place.

"Dad, is that your oldest daughter?" I cringe a little, hearing myself defer the oldest daughter slot I'd always thought was mine.

My father fingers the crumbling black paper behind the photographs, begins to turn the page.

"Please, Dad, is that Joanne?"

"Yes, it's Joanne." He turns the page and I see an attractive blonde woman with the slender dancer's legs my father had described. She is sitting next to a man with dark wavy hair who looks a bit like Clark Gable. I feel slightly embarrassed when I realize how handsome my father was when he was married to this stranger who is not my mother. The woman is holding Joanne in her lap.

"That must be Emily." I look over my shoulder to check in on my mother. She is rooted, silent. This must be the first time she has seen my father's other family. I suddenly want to protect her from the truth she has always known about my father's life, but perhaps never saw up close until now.

My father turns another page, and there is Joanne, about five years old, looking straight into the camera. She has a tentative smile. The hand-lettered sign in her lap reads "Merry Christmas, Daddy." My father is not behind the camera. He is probably behind enemy lines in the forest of Ardennes in Belgium, where he fought in the Battle of the Bulge. It could be any Christmas that he is overseas, but it must be the last, 1944, since Joanne was six by the time my father returned from the war, and in the heat of divorce, gave up his daughter for adoption.

What I feel for my father in this moment is compassion. I watch him turning the pages of his past, see a sadness in his eyes, in his hands, in the slowness of his movements, a sadness that he has never let me close to.

Looking at these photos, I realize that I know only a shadow of the man my father once was. Maybe none of us really ever knows our parents. At least parents who have been as unwilling to reveal themselves as mine. Still, I have always felt the urgency to know what lurked in the shadows, and now, watching my father mourn the loss of his first family, revealing a part of the shadow I never knew, I feel the fierce possessive wish that there had been no family before ours.

My father turns another page. There are several black corners with photographs missing. He turns around suddenly, and points his index finger at my face.

"You took these pictures out of here, didn't you?"

I shake my head, begin backing away. He jabs his finger into the air between us.

"You kids stole these—you, Paul, and David. I know you did."

"No, Dad, we never even saw the photo album—you yelled at us before we even got to it, remember?"

"Don't lie to me—"

After three more accusations, I stop backing up and plant both feet. I am twenty-eight years old, and I am not going to let him scare me.

"Dad, stop. You're imagining things."

My father drops his raised finger and slowly makes a fist. I no longer feel my feet. I brace for what is coming, close my eyes, then open them again. He drops his hand to his side and stares into the blank spaces where the pictures once were before closing the album.

"Well," my mother says, her first utterance since the album appeared. "Shall we try and find the box with your things?"

I take a deep breath, feel my feet again.

My mother and I begin the search for my boxes. My breathing slows down, and my father continues thumbing through the album. I recognize my handwriting on the top of one box, and we open it. My high school yearbook is inside— East High Wahina—and under it, a scrapbook filled with old track and field ribbons, a news clipping from the Wyoming *Tribune* about my winning the Cheyenne Symphony Young Artists Competition at seventeen, old music festival and competition rating sheets and judges' written comments. I pick out one of the rating sheets from a festival I played in at age thirteen, Beethoven's *Pathétique* Sonata, op. 13— "Exciting dramatic playing, but slow down—'con brio' does not mean a four-alarm fire."

The judge was referring to my playing of the first movement. I had always played it too fast. My left hand would start the eighth note octave tremolos at the Allegro di molto e con brio section and just go. I was always on the edge of losing it, but I raced through the whole exposition at top speed and made it all the way to the first Grave interruption before the development, grateful for the chance to slow down. The movement starts very slowly. The introduction is marked Grave. There is so much sustained tension from the first crashing C minor chord through the reserved *pianissimos* bursting into *fortissimos* that by the end of the introduction, after the long A-flat, the Allegro con brio section almost explodes.

I think it was my first musical introduction to sexual tension. I was feeling it all the time anyway, had just begun talking with girlfriends in whispered tones about the wet spot that appears in your underwear when a boy kisses you, and how you want to explode or something, and then later you do, with maybe a pillow between your legs while Paul McCartney sings "Michelle, ma belle."

Lucky for me then, and perhaps for every other adolescent who's ever performed Beethoven's *Pathétique*, Beethoven reinserted the Grave introduction (although shortened and transformed) just before the development and just before the coda, so you have two chances to catch your breath, to calm down. But then the tension rises with the sudden slowdown and it's like pulling way back on a slingshot, only to let it fly again.

"Some things haven't changed, Mom."

I show her the judge's comments.

"I'm still rushing—only now it's Symphony Hall instead of some podunk music festival."

"Marge, look," my father interrupts. He unrolls some old engineering drawings, spreads them out on the table with the photo albums and scrapbooks. "I really could do this."

My mother puts down the judge's comments and walks over to the drawings. I put down my scrapbook and clippings and follow my mother, feeling a bit dropped, but curious.

At first, the drawings look like blueprints, but when you put your finger on a line, it smudges slightly.

"Don't do that!" My father wipes my hand away.

I withdraw my finger and follow the precise pencil lines with my eye—indecipherable cylinders, squares, and arrows intricately drawn in perfect two-point perspective, with a cut-out slice of the drawing blown up. Measurements penciled in my father's uniform caps inform each arrow. There are blow-ups of drill holes and measurements written next to each. At the top of the drawing my father's name appears in perfect caps under the name "Allis-Chalmers, Milwaukee, Wisconsin" followed by a model number. My father lifts up the thin paper edge of the drawing to show us.

The tension of a few minutes ago is gone. It's as if my father has discovered some lost part of himself. He was a draftsman for a while after the war, but left engineering school at Marquette for seminary in Dallas after his first wife divorced him. Still, the draftsman never left him. I loved watching him draw at the kitchen table, which he sometimes did if he was feeling relaxed. When he was drawing, he would stick his tongue on the top row of his teeth and leave it there until the drawing was done. For a few minutes nothing else existed but my father's super-sharp pencil and pad on the kitchen table. I wonder if that was how he looked huddled over his drafting table. Sometimes he'd show us blueprints for the new church parking lot or the new bell tower. I was always amazed watching him walk around a building site, hard hat on his head, blueprints in hand, playing general contractor. I loved that part of my father. It was when he seemed most himself.

My father hands me a small black leather-covered box.

"Take this—it might come in handy if you ever decide to draw again."

I open the leather case and peer in at the shiny silver tools—mechanical pencils with little wheels on the sides, lead points encased in tiny silver holders, a silver compass and divider all neatly packed in black velvet. I see my father's initials, H.C., carefully penned into the little round label near the T-square insignia, and think of the pride he must have felt at owning his first set of nickel silver drafting tools. I run my finger across the velvet inside of the box and feel like I'm touching the best parts of my father. I wonder what made him trade these silver drafting tools for the silver chalice of the ministry.

Later, I lie on the bed in what was my sister's room, and reach over for the leather box, which is sitting on top of a small wooden cabinet next to the bed. This is the cabinet my father made for his mother in a high school shop class. It's cheap pine, but carefully inlaid with a few strips of cherry or mahogany. A yellow plastic kitchen cabinet handle is screwed into the door. My father said he couldn't afford a wooden one, so he took one of the extras from the kitchen cupboards. He was going to give the cabinet to Goodwill, but I've decided to take it with me. I stuff my old family slides, scrapbooks, yearbooks, and my father's engineering tools inside.

Later that day, while Karen and I divide up the music, she tells me she listened to the tape of the Mozart concerto I'd played with the Boston Pops.

"It actually made me cry, Lin," she says. "I picture you on stage with this incredible orchestra, and I can't believe it's my sister. I wish I could have been there."

I hardly know what to say. My sister and I have been enemies for so many years.

"Thanks," I say, testing the water. "I wish you could have been there, too."

"There's something else I have to tell you, Lin—"

My sister pushes her stack of music over to one side.

I'm waiting for the bomb to drop, the one that's going to explode this sweet peace between two warring sisters.

"Mom offered me the piano."

I feel a sudden sharp stabbing pain, but I don't look up at her. I continue sorting through piles of music.

"I said no, Lin."

"Well that was stupid. Maybe if you had the piano you'd start playing again."

"I *am* going to play again, in fact I feel inspired after listening to you, it's just—"

"Just what?" I ask, wishing I could take the hardness out of my voice, wishing I wasn't this worked up over a lousy spinet I grew up with that doesn't even come close in sound or depth to the Steinway I now own.

"I just didn't want it to come between us."

"Well, don't worry about it. I know you don't have a piano—"

"Dave and I can afford a better piano than that."

I put down my own pile of music, stand up and walk over to the piano. I run my finger along the walnut and brass music stand.

"It really is a lousy piano, isn't it?"

Karen stands up next to me and runs her hands along the keys. "Yeah, it really is."

I line up the fake marble statues of Bach, Beethoven, Chopin, and Brahms we'd earned for completing music theory exams with our teacher in Cheyenne, Mrs. Thamer, and turn them so that their white backs are facing us.

"You can have these," I say.

"No, I insist—you take them."

"Let's just leave them. The piano will look lonely without its mini composer busts."

I reach back into my music pile for the Dolly Suite by Fauré, and open to the first duet, "Berceuse." Karen and I stopped playing duets years ago because of turf wars. Her hands got bigger than mine, and even though I was a better pianist, I couldn't stand the possibility that she might pass me from behind. I sit on the left side of the bench, put my foot on the damper pedal. That's still my turf. "Let's try it."

"It's been too long. I don't know if I can play anymore."

"You take the primo part—it's easier."

My sister sits down next to me, and I watch her long fingers reach easily for the two high Es that begin the melody. "Promise not to play it fast?"

"Promise."

We begin the Fauré, and I half expect our brother David to barge into the room waving his arms to the music, which is what he did whenever Karen and I played duets. He must have felt left out, so he took over as conductor.

I think of a recital I gave two years ago, at the Hirshberg Gallery in Boston. It was a warm sunny day, and no one, including me, wanted to be inside. Mom and Dad and Vickie and little Dave were riding around in a swan boat at the Public Garden. But my brother, David, who'd missed my concerts at Jordan Hall and the Gardner Museum that spring, said he'd driven all the way down from New Hampshire to hear me, and even though he was the only one there, I'd better play something. I played the whole seventy-five minutes of music for him, Bach's Partita in G, the Bartók Sonata, Chopin's Ballade in F Minor and Schumann's Fantasy in C. At the very end, he stood up and clapped.

I wonder what he is doing now with those hands.

AUGUST 1992, DENVER

How do you know when you're done with an intrusive memory? They say it stops intruding.

How do you know when you're done with a hospitalization? They take you horseback riding. At least that's what happens here. There are six of us getting ready for discharge, five adults and one adolescent, and we're riding in the hospital van to the stables in Louisville, just east of Boulder.

On the way to Louisville, we pass fields of corn, sunflowers the size of your head, when the sharp purple outline of the Rockies appears against the huge blue sky. Toby, the kid from the adolescent unit, yells "Great!" and thrusts both thumbs into the air with equal zest at the sight of a falling down barn or a rusted out tractor. Great! to be out in the wider world, to be on the road, to be passing through long corridors between cornfields instead of the long corridors of a locked ward. But after about the twentieth time Toby yells "Great!" I look pleadingly at Larry, the leader in charge of group outings, who is sitting next to Toby. He puts an index finger to his lips.

Later, he informs me that Toby has Tourette's syndrome, a neurological disease that causes these outbursts, and that he, like me, has survived family violence and sexual abuse. Toby has come a long way from when he was first admitted to the hospital, Larry says. He used to yell "Fuck!"

I wonder if this is progress. If I'd yelled "Fuck!" when my father came into my room at night, I wonder if my mother would have paid attention. More likely, my mouth would have been washed out with soap. By the time I learned to use the word, I was ten. We'd just moved from Milwaukee to Cheyenne, and I was desperate to make new friends. When Greg Federer, Bobby Strasheim, and Rich Bedont told me to tell the fourth grade teacher, Mrs. Jackson, to "Go fuck a cow," I was too embarrassed to ask what it meant, and too anxious for approval to say no, so I did it. Walking by fast, I said it under my breath, but she didn't hear me. Greg, Rich, and

Bobby were leaning against the lockers, arms folded. I knew it wasn't enough, so I walked by again real fast. "Go fuck a cow!" I said, a little louder. This time Mrs. Jackson heard me, grabbed me by the arm and hauled me down to Miss MacNamara, the principal. Words flew about the new minister's daughter having such a foul mouth, and I was grounded for a week.

My father often swore around the house. My mother didn't like it, but as long as he didn't take the Lord's name in vain, she just rolled her eyes. I remember him calling the church organist a "fat sack of shit" more than once. So in eighth grade when I used the word *crap* over a drawing that was supposed to be in perspective and wasn't, I was surprised to get hauled off to the principal's office again. "You should be ashamed," my art teacher said, "a minister's daughter."

"My father says worse words than that," I protested.

"Your father can say whatever he wants in his own house," he said, "but I'll not have you swearing in my classroom."

My father picked me up that day, and to my surprise said he didn't think saying the word *crap* was any reason to get sent to the principal. I showed him the drawing I did that was out of perspective. He told me it was a good drawing, and knew exactly which side of the building was out of perspective and why. "I'll help you fix it," he said, "then next time maybe you should fart in his class." We both laughed so hard our eyes were watering.

. . .

Outside the stables, the van pulls into the parking lot and Toby yells "Great! Great!" like a record skipping. As soon as we're parked, I fling open the van door and embrace the quiet, punctuated only by crickets, a warm breeze rustling the leaves, and the neighing of horses in the barn.

After a lecture on safety, we are forced to don black velvet riding helmets with chin straps. After riding two-hundred and fifty miles on horseback through Bryce, Zion, and the Grand Canyon with only a Stetson on my head, I resent the helmet. Still, once we are led out to the stables where the horses are being tacked and saddled, my heartbeat picks up, my breath shortens. I am assigned Spicey, a spirited chestnut brown thoroughbred whose racing days ended only recently. She threw one too many riders. The riding instructor, an anorectic-looking blonde in her mid-forties, holds the reins firmly while I mount Spicey. I step up onto the mounting block beside the tall thoroughbred, take a deep breath, and stand a little taller next to her. Spicey snorts her approval. I place my left foot in the stirrup and throw my other leg over, center myself on the saddle, and wait. The instructor offers me the reins.

"If you can get her to do a collected trot all the way around the ring, you'll have done something," she tells me. "I warn you, though, hold her back, and don't let her lower her head, or she'll take off."

I nod and slap the reins lightly. It's a little like being given a Porsche and being told to keep it in second gear.

After one walk and two slow trots around the ring, I pat Spicey's neck. She's antsy. I can feel her neck twitching, tugging, begging me to ease up on the reins. The instructor gives the signal and I nudge her with my thighs, yell "canter!" and she's off. She accelerates, and I feel the long graceful strides beneath me. We head for the first low cavaletti. I give Spicey a gentle nudge with my knee and feel her massive body rise over the first jump.

Spicey tests me, pulls her head lower. I say "Whoa, girl," thinking "Go, girl," and pull up too quickly. She rears, then takes off at a full gallop, all fours off the ground, and races around the ring, passing all the other horses.

"Great!" Toby yells.

"Stop!" the instructor shouts, waving her arms. "Try the half-halt!"

I pull up short and quick on the reins, then release.

She slows to an even canter. I pull up and release again. She slows to a trot, and halfway around the ring, stable in sight, finally halts.

"Don't let her run—she *wants* to be controlled!" The instructor strokes Spicey's neck as if I have wounded her.

I struggle to believe her, but when I think of Spicey throwing that rider off her back, then running like the wind, I can't imagine her wanting to be controlled by anyone.

"What do you think this is, Bonanza?" she yells. "One more gallop in the ring and you're out of here."

We take three more slow trots around the ring, one canter and a jump over the low cavaletti, before I feel my own defiance, my own urge for speed taking over again. It's an old, old part of me, older than the first time my brother Paul let me take his motorcycle out. It was a Honda 900, and when I felt that huge rumbling engine between my legs, all that power, it was intoxicating. I took it around the block, then let out the throttle too fast in the home turn and skidded over onto my side, pinned beneath the huge metal beast. Paul came running out of the house to ask if the bike was okay. I was bloody and shaking, but I didn't care. I'd had my moment of letting go, the thrill and terror of letting the bike take over.

Now I'm fighting the wish to let go of the reins entirely, and let this horse do what she was made to do. I settle on letting go just a little. Spicey feels the slack in the reins, lowers her head, and picks up speed. I feel the thrust of the huge legs under me, the ground disappearing the way the road does when you are cruising at ninety. I imagine myself a wild riderless horse running through the open prairie, the mountains looming on either side. Suddenly I see the instructor running toward me, waving her arms.

"Sit back in your saddle!" she screams. "Pull up!"

I sit up tall, pull up the reins, and feel the shift between my legs from a full gallop to a fast canter. I feel the huge strength of this animal beneath me, and her resistance to slowing down. I pull the reins tighter and Spicey, reluctantly, slows to a collected trot. We pass by the instructor and she motions me over.

"That's it," she says. "Back to the stable." She takes the reins out of my hands and leads Spicey back inside.

"You should be ashamed," she says, "an experienced rider. Would you ever treat a horse of your own that way?"

"I've never had a horse of my own."

"Well, it shows."

Daddy promised to buy me a horse. When we were moving from Milwaukee to Cheyenne, I said I wasn't going. I said I would move in with Uncle Harry and go to school with cousin Nancy. She was a tomboy like me and the same age. Uncle Harry, her father, was a doctor. When I ran into the tether ball pole he sewed up my chin. When the ball smacked me in the chin a week later, he sewed it up again. If he could do that, I figured he could take good care of me. My grandmother and all of my cousins on my father's side lived in Milwaukee. For the first time in my life I felt the safety of family and I didn't want to lose it. I didn't understand until years later why we left. My father's ex-wife and daughter lived there. They went to the same church my Uncle Harry and his family attended. Emily, my father's first wife, was the Girl Scout troop leader for my cousins Nancy and Barbara. My father was afraid we'd find out. To quiet me down about the move, he promised he would buy me a horse when we got to Cheyenne. I remembered the piano promise, and how he'd come through with that, so with the horse promise in hand, I stopped complaining and sucked back my tears when the moving van came. We settled into our ranch house, and I cried every night for the first month. But I learned to love the treeless plains and the open, endless sky. And my father's promise comforted me. Every night I sang myself to sleep: "When you wake, you shall have all the pretty little horses. Dapples and grays, pintos and bays, all the pretty little horses."

I learned to ride that summer at Horn Creek Ranch in the Sangre de Cristo Mountains where we had church camp. When I got back, Janet Mathison, my new friend, let me ride her horse, Frosty. I told her my father was going to buy me a horse and soon we could ride together.

When I asked my father about the horse, he laughed.

"As soon as I start making as much as Colonel Mathison, I'll buy you a horse."

My father never mentioned his promise again. It was different from the piano promise. The piano was meant to shut me up for life. The horse promise was only supposed to get me out of Milwaukee quietly. Once we moved, it stopped mattering. I'd always felt a little strange about the promised horse, anyway. My mother was the real horse woman in the family. She'd ridden all of her life. If anyone deserved a horse, she did.

My father did other things to make up for moving us to a "hick town," which is what he called Cheyenne. He drove us to Denver about once a month just to remind himself and us of the big city. Usually he took us to a dinner theater, and I would laugh so loud during the funny parts of the play that my brothers would both give me dirty looks and my sister

Karen would sometimes just get up and leave the table. But my father, laughing hard too, and slapping the table, would lean over and put his arm around the back of my chair. On the way home he would defend me to the rest of the sulking family: "What's wrong with Linda's laugh? I enjoyed hearing it, and so did the actors. Did you see how they came right up to our table?" I felt uncomfortable when my father made a special case for me to my brothers and sisters, a little like Joseph when his father gave him the multicolored robe. His siblings wanted to kill him.

There were other privileges that came after we moved to Cheyenne. My father gave me the biggest bedroom in the house, which everyone, including my mother, never let me forget. But it meant that whenever company came, I had to vacate my room. Special favors always came with a price. I wonder what a horse would have cost me.

Inside the stable, I dismount, pat Spicey's neck, and walk over to sit on a bale of hay. Toby, who is not allowed to ride, walks over to where I am sitting, and yells "Great!"

"Thanks," I say, half-meaning it.

I walk out past the stables to a field of alfalfa. Storm clouds are gathering—so dark blue that the mountains and the sky are one—until lightning splits the horizon and disappears behind a ridge. Otherwise, the sky is uncut here—a few trees, the mountains, but mostly wide, flat plains and the huge expanse of blue. This is the sky I grew to love in Cheyenne, the sky that felt like an endless ceiling, the sky I would pray to more often than I ever prayed inside my father's church. I pray now, for the courage to go home.

Back at the hospital, Sandi is waiting to take me country western dancing at the Stampede. I have a pass for the evening, another chance to try life on the outside before I leave. Sandi is dressed in a flouncy little black and white flared miniskirt with ruffles on the bottom, a fancy white shirt with a silver bolo tie, and silver-and-white cowboy boots. My boots are plain black with silver flame stitching. I wear a plain silk shirt tucked into my jeans. I wouldn't be caught dead in prissy cowboy boots with a short skirt, even though Sandi looks great in them.

Maybe I'm a little jealous. I remember the way my brother Paul couldn't take his eyes off Sandi when he first brought her home. It will be the same way tonight, only it won't be Paul who's looking.

On our way out to her car, Sandi hands me an envelope—bills from home. I start to tear open the envelope, wondering how I'm going to pay them, when I remember what Dr. Grant said to me in my last session.

"Have fun this weekend. Put the hard stuff away. You're going to have to learn that in life. You might as well learn it here."

I stuff the envelope into my purse and open the door to Sandi's BMW.

"Let's dance, Lin."

Inside the Stampede, I see more cowboy hats than I've seen since the Cheyenne Frontier Days rodeo. The couples dancing the two-step swirl and float around the circular dance floor. It's like watching a cowboy ballet. Copland's *Rodeo*.

A guy named Trinidad, a friend of Sandi's, offers to teach me the cowboy cha-cha. I'm shy for many reasons—one, I haven't been touched by a man in so long, and two, I've never been good at following a man's lead. Sandi gives me a nod, and I say yes, feeling my back arch away from the hand that comes to lead me onto the dance floor.

The steps are simple, and since I'm a musician I know how to count, but when I have to follow I want to go my own way. Trinidad is slick, very polished. I can tell he's done this lots of times with lots of women. He takes me through a turn, but I don't come back to him.

"Hey—where do you think you're going?" he asks.

"Oh, sorry," I say, "I got carried away with the music."

"Just follow me, okay?"

"It would be better if you could just count out loud."

He winks at me, as if I were kidding.

I'm not.

"One, two, cha-cha-cha, step back, cha-cha-cha, that's it, cha-cha-cha—don't bee-bop—cha-cha-cha. S'posed to glide, cha-cha-cha—"

We switch to the easier two-step, and make it around the circular floor about three or four times, when I start to feel dizzy. I feel like a horse being reined in. This cowboy is the rider. My body is moving and spinning without me. The noise is beginning to enter my pores, not just my ears, and if I don't get to someplace to count, fast, I'll be a lost two-year-old with chattering teeth. I tell Trinidad thank you, excuse myself, and make a beeline for the bathroom.

When I get there and see the line, I feign a bladder infection and fling open the first stall door that opens. I sit down on the seat, flush the toilet, and start counting out loud from five to one. When everything is quiet inside me, and I'm back in my body and ready to walk, I go to the sink and wash my hands about ten times, then head out to the crowd and the noise.

Sandi spots me coming out of the restroom and waves me over to the dance floor. They're doing line dances, no partners. I think I can handle that. I pass by Trinidad, who's signaling me to the bar, wave back, and walk fast to the dance floor. I get in line next to Sandi and try to imitate her, crossing one leg in front of the other, stomping my boot.

"This is the electric slide." Sandi slides one foot toward the other, then stomps the heel of her boot into the floor.

I stomp the wrong foot and the music ends.

"The tush-push is next," she says, "but I've got to get you back to the hospital before your pass runs out."

After the tush-push and the achy-breaky, we are back inside Sandi's BMW. She asks me about Trinidad.

"He's a fabulous dancer, isn't he?"

"He's okay."

"You two looked great together." She looks at me sideways.

"Lin, you could really be a dancer if you practiced."

I feel like a fractured Cinderella. I made it to the dance, I ran away from the prince, I'm leaving with both boots on, and I can't wait to turn back into a patient.

JULY 1983, BOSTON

I'm taking the ferry to Nantucket for a lesson with Leonard Shure. Two and a half hours to study the score of Beethoven's op. 109, write in my journal, lie back, and feel the swell of the ocean beneath me. I am sitting on the upper deck, starboard side, feeling the salt breeze on my face, watching the gulls swoop down close to the railing for food. I'm writing in the journal Dan gave me for my birthday.

As resentful as he's been about my performing in the last two months—two concertos with the Boston Pops, five auditions in New York and Boston, three chamber music concerts with Boston Symphony players, a concert at the Gardner Museum—he's been oddly supportive of my writing. After concerts and auditions Dan gives me armfuls of flowers and stiff hugs, but I know he wishes I'd give up music and switch to something that's not what his mother does. Maybe writing.

The journal he gave me is clothbound, covered with branches of budding trees and flowers reaching upward. Inside, he inscribed lines from Emily Dickinson:

There is no Frigate like a Book
To take us Lands away
Nor any coursers like a Page
of prancing Poetry—
This Traverse may the poorest take
Without oppress of Toll—
How Frugal is the Chariot
That bears the Human Soul.

Dan introduced me to poetry during college. He was an English literature major, and I remember him sitting on his bed in his dorm room, leaning against the patchwork pillow I'd made him, in his brown flannel shirt, blond hair swept to one side, reddish beard making him look wise beyond his nineteen years, a book of poetry open in his hand. He was reading me one of his favorite poems by William Carlos Williams:

"So much depends
on a red wheelbarrow
glazed with rainwater
beside the white chickens."

"Yeah," I prodded, "go on—"
"That's it," he said, looking a little disappointed. "That's the poem."
"Oh. Well, read it again and maybe I'll get it."

He read the poem again, this time explaining the signifi-
cance of a wheelbarrow from a farming point of view.

His grandfather and father both farmed, and he'd run a
combine during summers in high school. He'd taken me out
to the farm in Fairfield to show me around. I remember the
huge red and white combines, lined up like tanks on the crest
of a hilly wheatfield.

"So much depends on an International Harvester Combine with an air-conditioned cab," I said, teasing him. "Especially given the hot summers and the size of your family's
wheatfields—"

I never "got" the red wheelbarrow, but I did ask Dan to
let me read whatever else he was reading. At the time he was
taking Russian literature, so I got my first taste of Dos-
toyevsky's *Brothers Karamazov* and Tolstoy's *Anna Karenina*,
which I loved best. That first line about unhappy families
drew me right in, and I didn't put it down until I'd said good-
bye to Anna's feet under the train.

Dan doesn't read to me anymore. His interests have
switched from literature to banking, and from flannel shirts
to gray flannel three-piece suits. We just took our first vacation since the bike trip last fall. One whole week on the Cape.
A little cottage in Eastham. On the beach, I watched Dan open
Henry Beston's *The Outermost House*. It was a glimpse of the
Dan I'd fallen in love with, and it made me hopeful.

But it didn't last. We spent most of the week fighting
over the fact that I'd found a little white church in Eastham

with a piano and was putting in three hours a day practicing. I didn't see what the big deal was in my disappearing for a few hours when we were spending so many hours together. Every morning we walked down to the beach and swam and had long leisurely breakfasts with *the New York Times* on our little deck. Dan rented a Sunfish and we sailed it around the bay. We windsurfed one day, then rode our bikes out to Nauset beach, where Dan taught me to skip rocks, something my brothers had told me only guys could do. We watched the sunset every night from the beach, on the bay side. Couples need time apart, I reasoned. Most afternoons while I practiced, Dan golfed, something I don't do anyway. I needed time with the piano, especially since I had this lesson with Shure coming up.

Still, every time I returned from practicing, Dan put up an ice wall that didn't melt until we sat on the beach to watch the sunset together. Sometimes even that didn't help, and he'd sleep with his back to me all night.

Maybe if I learn to write well enough, I can stop playing concerts and become a writer. A book of days could lead to a book of years, and I could write the story of my life. It could end happily ever after, two kids and a station wagon instead of two feet under a train.

But I'm not sure that would save my marriage. Dan told me the other night that no matter what I took up professionally, he'd be jealous. He says I'm married to the piano, and it would probably be the same with anything else I did.

The last night of our vacation, just before sunset, we walked down the beach to the salt pond. The tide was going out, and some of the fish that had swum into the pond to spawn were flopping around in the disappearing tide pool, unable to make it back out to the ocean. Without a word, Dan and I reached down and threw the struggling fish back out into the bay. As the water lowered further, more and more fish got caught in the sand. There were dying fish everywhere, their gills sucking in and out, and we couldn't rescue them fast enough. By the time the sun had vanished below the horizon, there were still hundreds of beached fish.

"Come on," Dan said. "It's getting dark."

"But what about all the dying fish?"

"They're going to die anyway. I'd rather not hang around and watch."

My brother David is missing. Three days ago he withdrew his life savings and vanished in his Toyota Celica. Vickie has not heard a word from him.

I almost canceled my lesson today, but I've been climbing the walls at home. I can't sit at the piano for more than ten-minute intervals. I pace from room to room like a caged animal. When the phone rings a terror seizes me. At first, I rush to get it, scream "Hello?" then make whoever called without news wish they hadn't. Yesterday, I moved the answering machine next to the piano and when the phone rang, I waited for my calmer, recorded voice to pick up. I'd sit there frozen until I heard the caller's voice, then when there was no news, I'd get up and start pacing. Dan finally told me just to go to Nantucket, take a break.

It's good to be hearing the lap of the waves against the side of the ferry and the squawking of gulls overhead. I take out my score for op. 109, but the little black dots swim on the page, and my mind drifts back to my brother David.

A few weeks ago, he drove up from Connecticut with Vickie and little Dave. We rode bikes along the Charles River and had a picnic there. David hardly spoke the whole time. After the picnic, we rode to a playground, and little Dave rushed to the tire swing.

"Push me, Daddy," he said.

My brother walked over to the swing, grabbed the rope and pushed with such force that little Dave flew out into the air, screaming like some terrified, wingless bird, then hit the ground hard. Vickie, Dan, and I rushed over to help him. Vickie scooped little Dave into her arms and held him while he sobbed. My brother just stood there, silent, morose.

I felt like I was watching a home movie: father hurts son, son grows up, becomes father, father hurts son.

"Don't take your anger at Dad out on him!" I yelled, immediately regretting it.

"I'm not angry at Dad," he fired back, "I'm angry at the world!"

"Well, you don't have to take it out on your son!"

Once little Dave stopped crying, we rode our bikes back to the house, hearing only the clicking of shifting gears and the squeaking of rubber brake pads.

Later, outside on the deck, I had a moment alone with my brother. He was smoking a Marlboro.

"I'm sorry I yelled at you," I said.

"Don't worry about it," he said, exhaling audibly.

"No, I mean it. Forgive me, okay?"

"Okay."

"I love you."

"I love you, too," he said, and for some reason, he let me hug him.

It's that conversation that scares me the most right now. I don't know why, but I feel like he was saying good-bye. It's what Paul did, just before hanging himself. He came to visit me at college the week before, visited our parents and sister in Texas, then went home and did it. For years everyone in my family has been telling me I'm not over Paul's death and that's why I'm scared about David. Isn't it reason enough?

I stare down at the open score until the first few measures of op. 109 come into focus, then start playing it in my head. Instead of getting interrupted by the diminished seventh chord eight bars in, the ferry whistle blows. I look up and see Nantucket Harbor. Leonard Shure is standing on the dock, smoking a cigarette.

I feel my breath shorten, thinking about playing op. 109 for Shure. Patricia Zander was the one who suggested it. She thought late Beethoven would be good for me. During my last lesson with her, we were talking about life choices, and she asked me if I really thought I could handle the lifestyle of a concert pianist, and if Dan could handle my doing it. "What if you're successful?" she asked. I said I didn't know how that would be, that Dan was already resenting it. Then she said that the people she knows who are happiest in life are the ones who really know what they want and are ruthless about going after it. They say yes to only what they want, and no to what they don't want. That's really what life is, she said, a series of yeses and nos.

I'm not the ruthless type, I tell her. I've been saying yes to music for most of my life, but I want to say yes to music without saying no to Dan.

That's when she suggested late Beethoven.

It's taken a long time to get the courage to actually play op. 109 for Shure. It's one of his banner works, which means he'll have even more definite opinions about the music than usual. If I express no opinion about the music, he'll jump all over me. But if I do express an opinion, I know it's going to be the wrong one.

I play the opening straight and accurate, the sixteenths as evenly as possible, the quarter notes in the right hand held through. I make it through the first eight and a half measures to the Adagio espressivo and play the diminished seventh chord before Shure stops me.

"No, no, no!" he says.

"No, what?" I say, hearing the edge in my voice. "I've only played nine measures."

"You just don't understand, do you?"

"Understand what?"

"The whole point of the piece."

"Well, hopefully there's more than one point—"

"My dear, if you already know so much, why are you here?"

For some reason I am more disrespectful than I've ever dared to be in a lesson with Shure. It must be my brother David. When I'm this scared, I get belligerent trying not to show it. This is the wrong piece to be working on with Leonard Shure when I'm this afraid.

"I'm sorry, Mr. Shure. I think I'd better come back on another day for this lesson."

"Don't be silly. You came all this way to study Beethoven with me, no?"

"No. I mean, yes—"

"So we begin."

Shure gives me one of the longest lessons I've ever had. Between all the yelling and starting and stopping, I forget my brother David for most of the time. But at one point, after I've played the opening for the twentieth time, I do what I vowed I would never do in a lesson with Shure. I burst into tears. Of course, it isn't Shure that makes me cry. Whatever thin membrane has kept a safe distance between the memories of my father's anger and Shure's snaps.

I am five, and my brothers and I are pulling our pants down, waiting. I am promising myself I won't cry, then I do.

Shure hands me a tissue from the table next to the piano. Clearly, I am not the first of his students to cry.

My father never handed me a tissue.

"Try the opening again," he says, "and remember, don't *be* it, *do* it!"

I look at the score. I see what Shure wants me to see: The first four descending notes, G-sharp, F-sharp, E, and D-sharp are the glue that holds this movement together, and what makes the Adagio espressivo section belong to the fast opening section—the same four notes recur in the right hand after the diminished seventh chord. But I can't get my fingers to reveal that. There is no connection between what I'm thinking and what I'm playing. It's as if my fingers are completely detached from my brain, limp and useless.

It reminds me of a game my sister Karen and I made up when we were little and played endlessly. Ragdoll. One of us would go completely limp and the other drag the limp one around the room. It's amazing how natural it was for both of us to turn limp and lifeless on command. But right now I can't command my body to come back.

Shure doesn't give up until I play the opening eight bars the way he wants them, which takes the better part of an hour. Just when I think the lesson is over, he moves on to the Adagio espressivo section, and the next hour is spent on the next seven measures.

On the ferry going back, I choose a seat that faces the wall, down under where the cars go, and cry most of the way to Hyannis.

There's news at home. Dan tells me David called and talked to Vickie's mother for almost an hour. Flossie begged him to come back. He's in Florida. He wouldn't say where.

For the next twenty-four hours, I can't stop moving. Perpetual motion. I can't practice, either. I decide to paint the deck. It needs a coat anyway. Dan and I are halfway through it when the phone rings. Dan gets it. I keep the paintbrush moving in long strokes until he comes back out and hands me the phone.

"It's your mother," he says, and I know from his eyes what the news is.

David was found dead at half past noon in a motel room in West Palm Beach. A three-fifty-seven magnum and two suicide notes were found next to him.

He'd shot himself in the head.

AUGUST 1992, DENVER

"The house is possessed," I tell Dr. Grant.

"The house itself was never the problem," she says, "it was the memories that surfaced there. You've already given up too much of your life for your father. Are you going to let him have the house, too?"

I am supposed to go home in a few days, but I'm not quite sure where home is. I'll be leaving the hospital, flying to Boston, and moving back into my house in Newton.

I haven't lived there since January 1991, when I opened the door to my house and smelled smoke. I saw black everywhere. The inside of my house was shrouded in soot. The oil furnace had imploded, covering the walls, the ceilings, the rugs, the furniture, the piano, all my books, clothing, and concert gowns with a black oily powder.

The fire on the inside of my house matched the fire that was smoldering inside me. In Baltimore, when I was little, my father shoved an altar candle into my face and said "If you tell you'll burn in hell." My brothers were standing next to me, stiff as statues. He pointed the candle at them. "Your brothers will die, too, and so will your mother."

Some very small, frightened part of me made the following deductions: I told. I had just written a letter confronting my father about the incest in early December. My mother stopped speaking to me on Christmas day, my brothers are already dead, and my house almost burned down. Next, he's going to kill me.

I decided to take my life first, with an overdose. I wasn't successful. I spent a month in the hospital. While I was there, I received a long letter from my mother. She wanted me to know that all four of her children had experienced a happy childhood, and that clearly, since I had attempted suicide, I was demon possessed.

"I may not have demons," I say, "but the house does."

"Since you're using art therapy so well, I want you to use it to make your house a safe place." Dr. Grant leans toward me from her chair, the way she does when she wants me to pay close attention. "If your house has demons, you'll have to find some way to exorcise them."

When I left the hospital in January 1991, it was clear that I couldn't return to my house. I spent the next seven months living with friends, aware that I needed them the way that I needed a family, but aware, too, of the burden I was placing them under to somehow make up for the family I'd lost, and to keep me safe from myself.

Dr. Grant says I need to take back my house in Newton, take back my own power. But how do you take back something you've never felt? I remember feeling powerful once in my life, when I was maybe ten or eleven. It was the time after my father stopped wanting me and before I got breasts. My mother says I was ugly. When I look at the photos—my brown hair pushed behind my ears, my bangs plastered down with tape to keep them from curling, my legs shapeless and gangly—I think she was right. I think she might have been relieved, too. My father hardly noticed me at all.

In that time I lived in a land without gender, and just for a while, I was me. I wore my brothers' clothes, their button-down shirts, which buttoned on the opposite side, and my cousin Laurie's hand-me-down dresses, which had darts I could smash down to make them fit. Everything fit and nothing fit, and nothing mattered because no one saw. When your father wants you in all the wrong ways, and then one day he stops for a few years before he wants you again, you grow up in a land without sex. That was when I felt the closest to God, the closest to powerful, and the closest to invisible. But how do you make the invisible visible?

I spend the next art therapy group drawing my house. It's a simple straight-sided mansard roof Victorian, so it's not difficult to draw. Not until I get to the windows. There's a ghost in every one. My brother Paul is hanging in the living room window. My brother David holds the gun to his head in the window next to that. I draw my own ghost in the bathroom, where I am emptying a vial of sleeping pills into my mouth. I draw my mother and father sitting at my kitchen window, Dan walking down the deck stairs to the moving van after we separated. There are ghosts of me at various ages in all the other windows—the two-and-a-half-year old, the five-year old with blonde curly hair, me at puberty, me the adolescent, and the me that still wants to end her life, standing in the window over the front door, a knife raised high over her head.

What surprises me is that, for all the hundreds of hours I spent practicing in that house, the piano is missing. There is music in the walls there, but the music has no ghost. Maybe it's the one purified element here that's meant to live on.

I draw my house again. Window by window, I send the ghosts out of the house. I draw them all floating upward, toward some kind of forgiveness.

Next, I draw an empty house, windows all blank. I draw myself sitting on the front steps, locked out.

"This isn't going to work," I say. "I can't imagine my house as a place I'd ever want to live in again."

"Try this," Trish, the art therapist, says. She hands me a big computer paper box with a lid—about twelve by eighteen inches. She hands me scissors, glue, and a pile of magazines—*House Beautiful, Better Homes and Gardens, Family Circle*.

I tear out photographs of beautiful rooms with massive windows and doors, and mountains overlooking green meadows, the sea with the sun dropping behind it, and as many skies as possible. I cut out doors, ceilings, and windows and paste what's left of the interiors over the sunsets, dawns, and starry nights. Every window, door, and ceiling is a painting that brings the outside in. I fill a fireplace with a mountain meadow, paste a cloudy sky inside a mirror. I paste a large goose waddling in through the front door, and inside the refrigerator, I replace the milk bottles with Holsteins grazing in a grassy pasture. Inside the kitchen, her elbows resting on a floating school desk, I paste a little girl. Looking up with a pencil at her lips, she is holding an open notebook, which now has a blue sky and clouds where the pages once were. She is some-place far away, imagining her life.

On the bottom of the box, I paste two halves of a house, completely split open to cloudless skies, evergreen trees, and a placid blue lake.

When I've finished, I show it to Trish.

"It's beautiful." She turns to look at all four sides. "I see all of the windows and doors look out—" She lifts the lid. "But inside it's still empty. Can you furnish that, too?"

I spend every free minute of my last few days in the hospital cutting and pasting. I cut out and paste in mothers holding babies, a little girl walking along a beach at sunset, holding her mother's hand, a mother and father bathing their baby together. There are young couples kissing, an old couple holding each other under an umbrella, a little boy peeking through a door at a bride, and a shiny black grand piano with a string of sixteenth notes pouring from the lid.

After I've finished pasting everything in place, I realize the piano is the only inanimate object inside the box, the only image that is not a relationship. Or is it? A therapist once told me you have to develop object constancy as a child to survive in this world, to know that one minute you may look up and see your mother is there and the next minute she's gone, but you know she's coming back. I never got that. The one object that has been constant throughout my life is the piano. I remember wanting and wanting my mother to hug me, comfort me, touch me, and butting up against the stony wall of her refusal. But there was the piano, a kind and patient mother waiting for my touch. There was no loss, no refusal. At six or sixteen, the piano was always there waiting.

But the rest of the images are wishes, both what I wish I'd grown up with and what I hope to share some day if I'm lucky enough to stay alive: marriage, family, possibly children, even grandchildren if I live that long. Maybe to imagine it is to begin it. To see it in detail is to begin living it, at least part time.

This box, I decide, is my house. A safe place to contain the past and perhaps to begin the future. I will take it back home with me, put it where I can see it before I go to sleep and when I wake up.

Still, the inside of the lid is bare. I make one more sweep through the magazines and find a woman in a green satin dress. Her brown hair is cropped close to her head, and her dark brown eyes are vacant. She is sitting side saddle on top of a white horse. She is not comforting, but something draws me to her. I cut her and the horse out, and snip off the reins. A few pages later, I find a tiny little girl with blonde curls. Her head is turned to one side and she looks afraid. I paste her onto the skirt of the green satin dress. I find a huge two-page photograph of a dark mossy cave and paste that into the lid of the box. I paste the woman on the horse inside the cave, with the little bit of light from the entrance behind her. She is riding into the darkness. On either side of the horse, I paste two doorways that open into the cave. Inside one doorway, I paste a man with a ranger hat and a searchlight. Above each doorway, I paste a child's hand reaching out, fingers spread.

I stop and stare at the woman on the horse. The ice queen. That's what I call her. I remember a photograph of the green satin dress my mother wore when she and my father were dating, and it strikes me that I have pasted my mother, only younger, into the lid of my box. But my mother's eyes are blue, not brown, and I wonder if the woman on the horse is really me. There is a part of me that pretends to need no one, and see no one, that cannot bear to be led by the reins any-where, but is unable to take the reins herself.

Kathleen Adams asks me to bring the box into my last journal group. She says we'll be learning to write dialogue between conflicting parts of ourselves. She wants me to write a dialogue with the ice queen, find out who she is.

At the top of my page I write:

Ice queen, who are you?

"I am the mirror, your mother, yourself. I give you the part of me that needs nothing, feels nothing."

Who is the man behind the door?

"There is no man. He's a figment of your imagination."

He's there. I see him through the door. He's holding a searchlight.

"I choose what I see. That is my power."

That's not power. It's blindness. The little girl in your lap—do you see her? She's reaching out her hands. She needs you.

"The child is dead."

Then you killed her, didn't you? You killed her, and now you don't even see her.

"Seeing only makes people afraid. I'm not afraid of any-thing."

I'll force you to see. I'll close you inside my box, hold your face to the poison and make you drink.

"I *am* the poison."

When I finish writing, I feel nothing. I show it to Kathleen.

"Very evocative," she says, "but you're not done."

The muscles in my neck tighten. I resent her judging this as real writing. This is only a hospital, I want to say, I have a real writing teacher in Boston.

"What do you think it needs? Plot? Character?"

"It's not what the writing needs," she says, ignoring my sarcasm. "It's what *you* need. The dialogue is a good beginning, but maybe you should try writing about whatever feeling the ice queen is helping you avoid."

"Like what?"

"Fear. See if you can write about that for a few minutes without stopping," she says, "unless it's too scary."

Afraid of appearing afraid, I go back to my seat. I write the word *fear* at the top of the page, then let my hand move across the page.

"I fear death. I fear dying. But worse than death, I fear the death of someone I need. My mother was always threatening to die. I feared her death the way she feared her mother's death. Her mother was always dying, always threatening to die. I fear my own death less than I fear my mother's. Death is a means of not having to fear her death anymore."

When I finish writing this paragraph, it comes to me: Just before trying to end my life in January 1991, I lost my mother. She wouldn't speak to me after I confronted my father about the incest. That made me feel she was dead. It's not that I hadn't lost her before. It's just that by that time, I'd lost most of the rest of my family, too. My mother had often spoken longingly of wanting to die. After Paul died, she told me she envied him. After David died, she said I should be glad he was in heaven with Paul and Jesus, and that she wished she were there, too. I told her I wasn't glad. I told her there was something terribly wrong in a family where all four children had such a strong death wish. Now two of us were dead. I said I didn't want to be the next.

When my mother visited me in 1990, I asked her about the incest in her family—the incident in Texas that made Grandma suicidal. She said she couldn't remember the incident, but then she didn't remember much of her childhood, so it wasn't a surprise.

During that same visit, I brought my mother to my writer's group. I'd just begun writing my novel, and since my mother loved to read, I wanted to share that part of my world with her. A woman in my group whose work was read that night was writing about hiding under the kitchen sink until her mother's crazy episodes were over. In a rare moment of candor, my mother said, "I understand what it's like to grow up with a mother who is mentally unstable." And just for a moment, I saw my mother, a frightened little girl, hiding under the kitchen sink until Grandma stopped trying to kill herself.

I take the box I made into my last session with Dr. Grant.

She lifts the lid and looks at the woman in the green satin dress.

"So this is the suicidal one."

She peers into the bottom of the box, at all the mothers holding their babies, the mothers walking with their children along a beach, the mother and father bathing their infant. There isn't one image without a mother in it, except the piano.

"She looks like she needs a mother."

"Who?"

"The suicidal one. You're going to have to learn to mother her."

Dr. Grant replaces the lid carefully, so as not to tear any of the pasted-on magazine skin, and holds the box in her lap. I want her to hold me there.

"This is the work you'll have to do when you leave here—in therapy, with your friends, in your house—you'll have to learn how to mother yourself."

I think of the long list of mothers I've had—therapists, teachers, friends, mothers of friends, my former mother-in-law, and for the longest time, the piano. It occurs to me that maybe that's where I'll begin. I'll go home and touch the keys, listen to my own sound the way a mother would listen for her infant's cry. Music is the language I understand best, where there are no words for the longing, where comfort comes at the fingertips, where a simple vibration disturbs the stillness in the air, lets you know you are not alone.

I need music. But I know I also need words. Giving a voice to what was once unutterable has saved my life.

Just before I leave the hospital, I gather with my new circle of friends—fellow patients, hospital staff, Dr. Grant. I play a hymn I grew up with, the one we heard Judy Collins sing at the Red Rocks Amphitheatre. And, like an old gospel revival meeting, we sing the words, "was blind, but now I see."

I feel the stillness I've felt just before beginning a concert, the stillness my father must have felt before opening his Bible to read from the pulpit, the stillness I must have felt before leaving my mother's body to greet the world.

Then I speak, hoping the words will take me home.

CODA

MARCH 1995, BOSTON

For the first time in three and a half years, I am playing the piano in public. It's a chance to help the relief effort for the survivors of the earthquake in Kobe, Japan, a chance to perform music I've always loved, and a chance to resume concert life, this time with a man who loves me, and loves my music.

Yesterday during rehearsal, the Steinway concert grand felt oddly familiar under my fingers. It was like coming home to an old friend and not recognizing the face, but knowing the smell, the touch, the sound of the voice. As I tried out the opening left hand triplets of the Rachmaninoff Prelude in D, op. 28, shifting the una corda pedal, listening for the softest, most unworn part of the hammer to strike the strings, I remembered: This is the Steinway that used to occupy the stage of the Gardner Museum's Tapestry Room. The Longy School of Music, where I now teach, bought this piano for concerts in Pickman Hall. The last time I played this instrument was almost ten years ago, when I gave a solo recital at the Gardner Museum.

Now I'm grateful to be returning to the concert stage with this old friend, knowing that it too, has endured change, the passage of time, and a number of moves. Tonight I am finally free to make music for its own sake.

The doors open. I walk out on stage, hear the applause, and feel a slight flutter in my stomach. I take a deep breath, bow, then sit, adjusting the bench until I am calm. I wait for the silence, for the music that fills my memory. When I finally feel I can take my time, I begin.